FATHER'S DAY

"The Age of Giving Back" was originally published in slightly different form in
Parents magazine.

Grateful acknowledgment is made to Warner Bros. Publications, Inc. for
permission to reprint four lines from "Over the Rainbow" by Harold Arlen and
E. Y. Harburg. Copyright © 1938, 1939 (Renewed) by EMI Feist Catalog, Inc.
Made in U.S.A. All rights reserved. Reprinted by permission of Warner Bros.
Publications, Inc., Miami, FL 33014.

Library of Congress Cataloging-in-Publication Data

McCoy, Bill.
    Father's day : notes from a new dad in the real world / Bill McCoy. —
1st ed.
        p.   cm.
    ISBN 0-8129-2405-3
    1. Fatherhood—United States.   2. Father and child—United States.
I. Title.
HQ756.M386   1995
306.874′2—dc20   94-23621

Manufactured in the United States of America
9   8   7   6   5   4   3   2
First Edition

FATHER'S DAY

NOTES FROM A NEW DAD IN THE REAL WORLD

BILL McCOY

TIMES T BOOKS

RANDOM HOUSE

To Amanda and Sharon,
and to Big Bill from Little Bill

ACKNOWLEDGMENTS

THERE ARE MANY PEOPLE TO WHOM I OWE A DEBT OF GRATITUDE for their wisdom and morale-building powers. Some of them probably don't know they've been so helpful. Quite a few of them appear pseudonymously in the text, others openly and without shame.

These folks include: Jacquie and Tom Rogers, Jeffrey Abrahams, Don Wallace and Mindy Pennybacker, Richard Louv, Dr. Lawrence Kutner and Cheryl Olson, Angela and Hank Bennink, Don and Kimiko George, Chris Hunt, Robin McMillan and Gail Heimann, Dave Dunbar and Barbara Peck, Patty Cook and all the Gallaghers, Wayne Kalyn, Vicki Secunda, Ibrahima Traore, Michael Wolff, Anthony Weller, Jon Spayde, Elizabeth Bibb and Mike Yamashita, Bob Kotlowitz, Sandy and Ernie Janssen, Jane Dalzotto, Eleanor

Robinson, Harold Christian, Bill Cross and Carole Francesca, Ed and Hedy Campbell, Kevin Cobb, Joe Gioia, Father William Guerard, and Florence from the bus—who told us when Amanda was still in the womb that "a baby brings its own good fortune," and turned out to be 100 percent correct. I'd also like to thank all the children of the people listed above for making the parents among them such good ones.

It's hard to say enough good about all the people I work with at *Parents*, but in particular I'd like to thank Ann Pleshette Murphy, my editor-in-chief, who has been as helpful, steadfast, and understanding a boss as anybody could hope for. I also appreciate the moral and technical support as well as the uncommon wisdom of Wendy Schuman and John Wehba.

I am deeply indebted to Henry Dunow, my agent, who has believed so strongly and steadfastly in this book that he often revived my own confidence. The book's editor, Betsy Rapoport, is largely responsible for imposing whatever order and clarity it possesses, as well as making the collaboration genuinely enjoyable.

And then there's family. My sister and brother-in-law, Betsy and Doug Hornberger—and their thoroughly wonderful daughters, Jennifer and Allison—were instrumental in inspiring Sharon and me to start a family, so we owe all four of them big time. My mother, Marjorie McCoy, has been an unending source of candid good sense and love, and I am more thankful to her and for her than I could ever express. Many thanks also to my mother-in-law, Amanda Alcala, who in her quiet way may be the strongest of us all.

Finally, it would be unthinkable not to mention my late father-in-law, Elmer Alcala, one of the most decent, intelligent, and life-loving men I've ever known—and one of the funniest, too. If anyone I ever met truly was a great father, he was the guy.

CONTENTS

CONTENTS

INTRODUCTION

LET ME REASSURE YOU RIGHT AWAY ON A CRUCIAL POINT: I AM NOT a fatherhood expert. I have done absolutely no postgraduate (or even undergraduate) work in child development, psychology, or any technical field even remotely connected with the subject.

My only claims to knowledge on the matter are my two jobs. One is as personal assistant to the nearly two-year-old combination cherub and spitfire I am delighted to call my daughter. The other is as an editor at *Parents* magazine—and the only male one, which makes me sort of resident dad there. Fatherhood, then, is a topic that occupies most of my time, even when I'm not hanging out at home with the more demanding of my employers.

This isn't a how-to book or a "humorous" collection of

dyspeptic one-liners. And don't expect to be told in these pages why the American dad is emotionally crippled and desperately needs to get back in touch with himself. I have nothing against reflection—it's a great thing as long as you don't spend too much time in front of the mirror. But it seems to me that the kind of guy who really needs to take stock of himself is rarely someone who reads books.

So this isn't about *how* to be a father. It's more about *what it's like* to be a father. And what is it like to be a father? Actually, on the whole, it's pretty damned wonderful.

Whether you have kids or not, a lot of guys out there—often the ones who've always got great excuses for not starting their own families—will tell you that men who really enjoy being fathers have irrevocably dropped the flag and surrendered to domesticity. Someone needs to tell these boys that the alarm clock is ringing. Adolescence is over.

Not that becoming a father guarantees instant contentment. You're unlikely to be bowled over by this next observation, but parenthood isn't what it was even a decade ago, largely because, like it or not, the one-income family has gone the way of the vinyl LP. As our wives assume a larger presence in the working world, we dads are assuming more of a presence at home. It's that simple.

Still, it's easy for new dads, upon first discovering this, to feel cheated. Why can't we just drive off in the morning, do our jobs all day, then return to preside regally over a home-cooked meal before disappearing into our newspapers, the way our fathers did? Modern fathers who can't adjust to the facts start to resemble those stereotypical upper-class Brits who haven't quite brought themselves to believe that the sun has set on the Empire.

If the world of our fathers has pretty much vanished, what do we do now? Might I suggest that we not only accept but embrace the inevitable?

Of course, fatherhood is hardly pure duty. As exhausting and anxiety-intensive as this business can be at times, my daughter has also provided me with more unmitigated fun than anyone I've known since my own early days. (With the exception of her mother, of course.) Becoming a parent has given me a second childhood—and a first adulthood. I am grateful beyond measure for both.

Since I began writing this book, I've been lucky enough to find a few fathers who feel more or less the same way I do, and who have been glad to swap ideas and stories. It has also become clear to me that there are a lot of new dads who'd love nothing better than the chance to shoot the breeze with another new dad—somebody with whom they could compare notes, maybe even get a little philosophical midway through the second beer.

I'm not saying we have to break down into confessional puddles in front of each other—I'm not exactly the encounter group sort, anyway. But it might be helpful if we knew what was on each other's minds.

So this book is intended to start that conversation. It's nothing more than a new dad's attempt to make sense of his role. And to explain why he is convinced that fatherhood is, as it always has been, the express lane to the greatest happiness a man can possess in life.

FATHER'S DAY

ENTER AMANDA

If ever a child had a boring birth, it was our daughter.

Of course, by definition a birth is never boring to a parent, except maybe to one who's extraordinarily jaded or heavily anaesthetized. (Either gender.) Nonetheless, the glorious mystery of Amanda's passage from the pre- to the postnatal world was hardly Movie-of-the-Week material. Apart from a handful of small surprises, an example or two of gallows humor, and several moments of tension, its most notable feature was the stolid, inexorable flow of events toward a conclusion that was basically—though not entirely—predictable. Like I said, boring.

Still, I'll take it. With gratitude.

Sharon was four days overdue. I'd stayed home because she was scheduled to see her obstetrician that afternoon and couldn't drive herself. Besides, the night before, having gotten tired of waiting, we'd gone to Plan B. I'd heard a dubious piece of folk wisdom that spicy food can trigger labor, so with my wife's full consent, I whipped up a dinner of Korean beef surrounded by murderously hot condiments. We were only mildly surprised when her water broke promptly at noon the following day.

"Must have been the Korean beef," I said.

"After that dinner, she's probably desperate to escape," Sharon said. (We already knew she would be a she.)

We showed up punctually for the doctor's appointment and found that, sure enough, labor had begun. The obstetrician told us more or less the same thing everyone in our position is told—when the contractions get to be five minutes apart and last for a minute apiece, it's time to call the answering service. Driving back home, I asked Sharon what it felt like, if it hurt much. She didn't appear to be in a lot of pain. "It's sort of like having a mild period," she shrugged. "Of course, it only started a few hours ago."

We had dinner, watched *The Simpsons*. I kept a log of the contractions, exactly as a dutiful Lamaze graduate is supposed to. Sharon made up little bags of Halloween candy "in case I don't feel like doing it when I get home." (As Halloween was only two days away, this seemed a little casual, even to me.) Every hour her contractions drew a little closer together and lasted a little longer, just like we were told they would. The situation seemed eerily under control.

"So far it looks like we're going to be like the first couple," I said. In our final Lamaze class we'd seen a movie of three births. Just so nobody would panic, I guess, the film opened with a delivery so ridiculously hitch-free that unless you were really paying attention, you couldn't even see any blood.

"That's not funny," Sharon said. She meant it.

By the time the eleven o'clock news was coming on, the contractions had reached the critical stage. The pain was serious. So I called the answering service; Sharon's doctor wasn't on hospital duty, the calm lady at the other end said. However, she'd call the doctor who was and he'd call back within five minutes. Meanwhile, the labor's momentum was quickly picking up. I abandoned the chart—it seemed sort of like telling your diary how it felt to be on the *Titanic*. A half hour later, with Sharon barely able to walk, I dialed the service again. The calm lady at the other end said she'd just spoken with the doctor, who'd inadvertently switched his beeper off. He passed along his apologies and suggested we head over to the hospital right away. This, I felt, represented the acme of sound thinking.

We were nothing if not prepared for the journey. The tank was full of gas, the tires were brand new. It was midnight, so a traffic jam wasn't in the cards. Even so, I was in a state of barely suppressed panic in my eagerness to get to the hospital. My nerves had nothing to do with the possibility that we might arrive too late—in fact, that might have been the only thing I wasn't terrified about. What unnerved me most was that we hadn't encountered a real crisis yet. I kept looking for the telltale signs of impending disaster, but impending disaster refused to cooperate.

At a stop light a car pulled up next to us. The driver rolled down his window and said politely, "Excuse me, can you tell me how to get to Route 1 North?"

I suddenly had a vision of our daughter entering the world while I was attempting to point some guy with Virginia plates toward Piscataway. After several moments of frantic thought, I suddenly remembered—we were *at* the intersection of Route 1. "My wife is giving birth! Turn right!" I yelled just as the light changed. I hit the gas, and plowed through the intersection.

We got to the hospital just after midnight—in time, and in luck. Our delivery room was the "homey" one. That meant that instead of being icy, clinical, and filled with stainless steel, it looked like an unusually clean economy motel room, down to the solid beige wallpaper and paint-by-numbers still life. The only difference was that motel rooms generally don't come equipped with fetal monitor hookups approximately the size of Eric Clapton's amp.

Sharon got a shot of something designed to take the edge off her contractions, theoretically enabling her to rest up for the effort ahead by grabbing a series of thirty-second naps. In the meantime, I set up camp in a diabolically uncomfortable and slippery plastic armchair. My brief, in accordance with Sharon's wishes, was to serve if called upon, but otherwise to remain well in the background. Not that my presence in the delivery room was unwelcome, mind you. However, as she said to me in the car, "Unless you can find a way for me not to feel as if my insides are about to explode, there's really not a whole lot you can do."

Because we'd been forewarned that a lot of dead time was likely to precede the serious work, I figured it would make sense to try to keep at least one of us amused. So I brought along my Walkman and some tapes, as well as two or three books, a few cans of soda, and a large bag of potato chips. It's a wonder I didn't toss a badminton set and an outdoor grill into the hatch as well.

Nonetheless, after a halfhearted attempt to munch a few chips and lose myself in Otis Redding's greatest hits, my toys were relegated to a side table, where they sat untouched. Instead, three A.M. found me huddled in the near dark, listening to Sharon's uncomfortable breathing as well as the impossibly slow, hypnotic swishing of her amplified heartbeat coming from the fetal monitor. Occasionally I checked the small lighted screens to make sure her contractions were staying regular, or got some ice chips at her whispered request. Apart from that, I was little more than a night watchman. Once I tried to help her breathe; kindly but firmly she said, "I know you're trying to be useful, but you're throwing me off. You'll get your chance to help."

So what I ended up with was a lot of time to think. Primarily I thought about fairly basic things—like how we were both really here and how it was all really happening. And that by the time this day was over, Sharon would be a mother. Moreover, I would be a father. And I would never *not* be a father again.

This concept wouldn't have been nearly as frightening if I'd had the slightest idea of what being a father meant. Except that I was leaving non-fatherhood behind, and I wasn't really sure what *that* was, as I'd never known anything else. Was our daughter going to like me? (I felt pretty sure I'd be nuts about her.) Was I going to follow in the path of a few of the guys I knew who turned remarkably stuffy the moment they became parents? Would I find the sheer inescapability of fatherhood suffocating? Would I inadvertently start using the kinds of phrases—"Righto, sport" or "So help me God, if you *ever* . . ."—that used to make my skin crawl when my dad used them with my sister and me? Would Sharon and I start calling each other Mom and Dad, and forget to go back to our real names when the kids left home?

I knew the club I was leaving behind, but didn't know the one I was about to join. All I could really do was sit in that unbelievably quiet, ugly room wondering what the rest of my life was going to be like. When it all got to be too much, I did what any man in my position would do: I went for more ice chips.

There's no need to recount here the full story of how Amanda came to be born. The pushing and all that, I mean. That's really my family's story. Not that it's off-limits, but there's no way it could be interesting to anyone else. Suffice to say that Sharon was eventually fully dilated, that two labor nurses and I did everything we could—not much compared with what Sharon had on her job sheet—and that the final outcome took a long time because Amanda was an astonishingly large baby, an ounce short of ten pounds. There were no real complications or moments of high drama, just a lot of work. Amanda Katherine McCoy was born around eight-thirty in the morning of the newest day ever.

Sometimes people ask me what I felt the first time I saw my child. At first I didn't know how to answer. By definition, when you're emotionally overwhelmed it's impossible to sort out the constituent emotions. And on top of being over-whelmed, I was also bone tired and more than a little dis-oriented—so much so that it took a few moments to even register that what the labor nurse was waving in my face was indeed our daughter.

Yes, I felt love for the purplish-red, slime-covered beauty queen in front of me, and maybe even more for the miracu-lous woman who had just delivered her. But beyond that? Delight? Awe? Tenderness? Terror? A little bit of all those things, but also something else it took a few months for me to find the name for: inevitability. If there was one thing about which I was absolutely sure at the moment I saw my daughter, it was that we were meant to be together, all three of us. Maybe my brain waves were warping a little at that moment, but I thought I saw the same recognition flickering in her eyes as well.

Apart from that, all I can recall is being just lucid enough to know how numb I was. There was all kinds of stuff bouncing around in my brain and my heart that I knew wouldn't be unearthed for days, weeks, maybe years.

Meanwhile, there were practical matters to be addressed. Finally, I could *do* something, sort of. For the next three hours I was on autopilot. Most of the time I hung around the prep nursery, where our daughter aced her Apgar test and gave such a convincing demonstration of the sucking reflex that she nearly removed the skin on my pinky. She also bore with surprising patience my frazzled attempts to get just the right camera angle for her first photograph. It took several minutes before I found a composition that seemed to do her justice; and all the while she simply lay on her side like a chaste odalisque, expectant and slightly puzzled about all the fuss I was making.

Then I'd make an appearance back at our suite at the Maternity Inn, where a recently stitched-up Sharon was calmer and more businesslike than I'd ever have imagined. She asked for details on Amanda's movements, disposition, even eye color, in a manner better suited to a tax auditor than a new mother. It was as if she'd told herself, "Okay, now *that's* out of the way. Time to roll up our sleeves and get to the *real* work." I didn't realize until the moment was upon us how much she wanted to be a mother. I don't think she did, either.

We traded a few notes on the delivery, mostly remembering what we or the obstetrician or the labor nurses had said at various points, piecing together Amanda's story for posterity. I wanted badly to tell Sharon all the things I couldn't even articulate for myself. But even if I'd known what to say, she was too physically spent to listen. Just about the only thing we knew—and I'm not sure how we knew this, but it was utterly certain that we did—was that we suddenly had a lifetime's worth of things to tell each other, and probably wouldn't ever get to them all. She finally said, "You really have to go home. You need to sleep almost as much as I do."

On the way back, I sort of mentally split into three people. The first drove. The second one sat in amazement that the first one was able to drive. The third one tried to compose a message to put on the answering machine once all three of us got home. He failed utterly. My mother, sister, and several friends tell me the message I ultimately left was very coherent and charming, considering that its author appeared to be someone in an advanced stage of delirium.

I honestly don't remember what I said. All I remember is going to bed in the middle of the afternoon with my head spinning, feeling as if I'd been beaten up by angels.

COMING CLEAN

Decades from now, when my wife and I hash over the high points of our first years with Amanda, I'll depend on Sharon to mention her first smile or her first tooth or her first steps—even that memorable first birthday party, which concluded with Amanda's gleeful trashing of an entire chocolate cake. (It didn't occur to her that she was supposed to eat it.)

I won't be thinking about any of those things. No, what I will recall most fondly from the early days of fatherhood is bath night.

Sharon gets things started by running the water while I get Amanda undressed. I don't think it hits her that she's about to be bathed until her head pops out of the little undershirt and she's naked. Then she makes a wild, happy little screech and lurches for me, arms outstretched. I can't decide whether it's because she's delighted not to have any clothing on or whether she realizes that a treasured ritual is about to begin. I lift her in the air so that she almost touches the ceiling, and she wriggles and screeches some more.

By now the water is ready. Her throne with the suction cups on the bottom sits in the middle of the tub, surrounded by a froth of bubble bath and a flotilla of cups and ducks and fish and round little people who fit into plastic turtles. As I lower her into her seat, she stretches out her arms and points her toes, almost as if she's diving.

We don't get into the actual washing right away. What's the hurry? Instead we warm up with some preliminary splashing. All I need to do is give the water a few tentative pats, and in an instant she becomes Keith Moon, launching into a particularly strenuous and deranged drum solo, except I don't think he ever shrieked with pleasure quite so earsplittingly. The water slops and whooshes and capsizes all the bath toys, and bits of bubble fly madly through the air. Like most activities undertaken by one-year-olds, this doesn't last long. However, for its duration it is distilled joy.

When peace returns to the tub, I fill an orange plastic cup and wet her back and arms, then lather up the washcloth and run it gently over her upper body. Having momentarily expended every ounce of her energy, she complies, shivering a little as the rinse water cascades over her shoulders. Then I shampoo her. A little revived by the scalp massage, she strikes a duck and a turtle together, pretending they're cymbals. I give her a unicorn hairdo, like the Ed Grimley character from the old *Saturday Night Live,* then a Jetsons pompadour. Even without my arsenal of TV reference points, she knows she looks pretty hilarious, because this is often the point at which her mom saunters into the bathroom and starts cracking up.

When Sharon leaves, I say, "Tilt your head," and immediately—if not with great eagerness—Amanda grips the sides of her seat and tries to lean back. She's not quite coordinated enough to pull it off right now, so I delicately cup her chin. Her eyes look imploringly at the ceiling as if she is beseeching the fates to keep soapsuds out of her eyes. As the water showers through her hair, she sucks in her breath; had I not put my fingers beneath the faucet to make sure of the temperature, I'd swear I was pouring glacier water down her neck.

Still, I tell myself, she's facing up to small discomforts well. She may dramatize them a little, but she hangs in there. That's a good sign. To reward her bravery, I initiate another round of splashing, which she takes up with vigor.

Soon the water cools and she starts to look a little grayish-yellow—the tip-off that it's time to wrap up this production. I give her face the once-over, then lift her from her throne for a quick but vigorous scrubbing of her toes, feet, legs, knees, and popo. (I know you're supposed to use correct names for body parts, but I happen to like the word "popo.") As I wash each body part I announce it, trying to sound like the guy introducing the orchestra in "Tubular Bells."

Then I deposit her carefully on the towel in the middle of the bathroom. She immediately locks into the fetal position. I pick her up, and her hands reach out. She wants to be held, but her body is frozen in its crab-like posture. However, she soon begins to thaw, and by the time we've reached her room she's plastered to me. I am not, if the truth be known, in a huge rush to lay her on the changing table and dry her off.

But being a conscientious servant, I get around to it, albeit in a leisurely way. Once she's toweled off, I knead in the moisturizer, and slip her into her pajamas. She's so mellow from the warm bathwater and the exertion that she can barely lift her arms to get them into her sleeves. I comb her hair so that the ringlets fall behind her ears. And then comes the best part: I bury my nose in the crook of her neck and take the deepest breath I can.

There, just beneath her skin, is Amanda's special perfume, compounded of soap and fresh biscuits and honey and pears, as well as the earthy aroma of wet hair. But there's something else, something indefinable, something that is simply the scent of a newly washed child. It's a smell no parent can ever forget.

At some point during the hair-care portion of our ritual, Sharon has stolen into the room and left a bottle of milk on the night table. Amanda can barely keep her eyelids from fluttering shut as she struggles to finish it. When she finally does, I lay my inert bundle of child into her crib and start away. It's time for me to slip back into the world.

But before I do, there's one more duty that must be carried out. I lean over and fill my lungs with my daughter just one more time.

SURVIVING OUR BLISS

There's a couple we know who have on at least two public occasions—and without seeming provocation—mentioned in loudish voices that the arrival of their first child produced no discernible strain on their marriage, and that parenthood left their love for each other utterly intact.

Call me jaded, but people like this remind me of a guy I once met at a party who swore he dropped LSD roughly once a week for six and a half years without any psychological or emotional damage whatsoever. In both cases, it is technically possible that the people involved are not delusionary. In both cases, not for a second do I believe it.

The introduction of a baby into a couple's life is too complicated and profound a thing not to have some destabilizing effects in addition to the many deeply gratifying ones.

There isn't a marriage I know that hasn't undergone a fundamental alteration practically from the moment the little strip turned blue. And I'm not talking about a testy period that goes away after a few weeks. The birth of a child has already played a major role in breaking up one good friend's marriage.

Nor will I soon forget the night an old college pal confided to me, when he was a couple of beers past the point of discretion, that he was on the verge of leaving his wife and their baby. "I don't know who Elaine is anymore," he whimpered. (That, obviously, is not her actual name.) "She used to be Elaine, but now she's a *mother*. Even to me. Her mom was a general, and now she's a general, too." He never did carry through on his threats to bail out, and I sometimes wonder whether it was because he was only speaking out of a momentary despair, and he took a clearer-eyed view of his life a little later on and saw what an asinine thing he'd be doing.

Whatever the reasons, I have not quite forgiven him for making this confession to me three weeks before Sharon's due date. He played right into one of my most persistent pre-fatherhood fears—that becoming a parent wasn't so much a matter of gaining a child as losing a wife.

It's easy and tempting to assume that any shift in married life caused by children is going to be a bad thing, especially if you were pretty happy with your spouse before you thoughtlessly set the wheels of change into motion by impregnating her. Certainly my love for Sharon—which, before Amanda, I considered impervious to anything short of nuclear attack—has endured more than a few shaky moments in the months following the birth. There have even been several times when I've wondered whether our marriage would survive the bliss of parenthood. And it's pretty clear I wasn't the only one wondering.

If I appear, as this chapter progresses, to be holding back on the really intimate stuff, it's not because I'm embarrassed or afraid of the consequences. It's because the details of our story aren't, to be perfectly honest, likely to land us on *Geraldo* any time soon. (Darn.) Any errors I might make on the side of discretion come out of a desire to preserve at least a semblance of my family's privacy, while also keeping anyone reading this from breaking out in hives from sheer boredom. The only reason for telling as much as I do is to demonstrate that if our marriage could be stretched close to the breaking point, anyone's could.

We are, as I say, private people. However, I think Sharon would have no objection to my mentioning that of all the women I know, she is the smartest, funniest, most generous, most down-to-earth, most openhearted, and most sensible. The fact that in a little black dress she's an inspirational sight is strictly coincidence.

But none of these virtues were what first won my heart. Her appetite did that. On our second date, I took her to one of my favorite restaurants, a dirt cheap place in a dodgy neighborhood. (Come to think of it, *all* my favorite restaurants back then were dirt cheap places in dodgy neighborhoods.) The food was more or less Pakistani home cooking. When I saw her delighted and vigorous—though never less

18

than ladylike—assault on a shrimp biryani, it became immediately obvious that this was a woman I could grow old with. Later that evening, she not only laughed at the vilest joke I knew but told me one that was even worse. The deal was sealed.

What has sustained her love for me over the past fourteen years I wouldn't even try to guess. It's not that I feel unworthy. It just seems like one of those things you're better off not knowing. I'm just grateful for it.

Before Amanda came, we lived a well-ordered life together and enjoyed each other about as much as I imagine two people can. Rarely did we ever raise our voices—not because we were seething cauldrons of repressed anger, but because we hardly ever disagreed. And when we did, we could generally air our disagreements in a normal tone of voice, the other person would listen, and the issue would somehow be resolved. Edward Albee wouldn't have found much to admire in the relationship, but it worked for us.

I remember once having a drink with a male friend who'd been very happily married to the same woman for thirty-odd years. I told him that sometimes I felt as if Sharon and I were more like brother and sister than man and wife. "Exactly," he replied.

In the days immediately following Amanda's arrival, Sharon and I lingered in that postnatal afterglow that is part shock, part exhaustion, and part apprehensiveness, but is mostly the sweetest sort of awe at the fact of having an infant around the house. It wasn't clear to either of us yet that things between us had become different. However, as parenthood's initial novelty began to wane, and we had to accustom ourselves to the idea that life consisted of more than just Amanda, we took a close look at one another again. When we did, we suddenly felt like occupants of a house that had been snapped in two by a cyclone, with both halves swept into the air and deposited in different counties.

Part of the problem was, of course, sexual. Though I'm still not sure Sharon entirely believes me, I considered her just as physically desirable as she'd been before having a child. However, I have to admit that my randiness *had* been dampened by the spectacle of birth—but not for the reason you might assume. Amanda's delivery was so emotionally powerful that, having witnessed it, I felt I'd never be able to take sex lightly again. Even after Sharon's obstetrician gave us the go-ahead at her six-week checkup, I had great difficulty summoning the appropriately frolicsome mood. It was as if I'd found out that the playground where I'd been cavorting for the last dozen years was actually a religious shrine.

Further complicating the physical angle in our relationship was a problem that was a lot more prosaic, but just as hard to overcome. With our decision to install Sharon as the full-time parent, I was starting to feel the pressure that goes along with being Mr. Income. It's sad but true: When you're trying to figure out which bills can wait a month so that you can get your pediatrician paid, neither bringing another person to orgasm—no matter how dearly you love her—nor achieving it yourself is quite the priority it once was. Especially when the fruit of a previous coupling has just managed to drift off to sleep in the bassinet five feet away from you.

In fact, in those first months I would often wait to be certain Sharon was already asleep before I came to bed. I didn't like avoiding her, but I was determined that she not find out how much of an effort it took to get to sleep each night, how wrapped up I was in worry over money. Ducking the conjugal bed until your wife is slumbering does have a way of curtailing your sexual activity.

But the largest hurdle had nothing to do with either sex or money. It was our discovering that the relatively straightforward give-and-take of a two-person relationship became immensely more complicated when a tiny third party entered the picture. Instead of each of us putting the other's interests first—which had always been the cardinal rule of our old life together—each of us gave the pole position to Amanda. Which was, of course, exactly as it should have been.

But now it seemed as if every single drop of my emotional energy was being channeled into the exhilaration and pride and tenderness and anxiety I felt about my daughter. When I got home from work each evening in those first few months, I'd make a beeline for her, and for the next hour or so I lived exclusively in her world. Only when Amanda was conked out in the bassinet would I change out of my coat and tie, come downstairs, and kiss Sharon hello.

If anything, Sharon had less of herself to spare for me. She was as emotionally poleaxed as I was, and at the same time treating her new role with even greater seriousness. Her zeal for motherhood and determination to do it right were both surprising and genuinely affecting to see. However, the high standards and attention to detail that served her so well in, say, decorating the nursery were harder to find charming

21

when she applied them to matters such as the amount of balm I used on Amanda's behind while diapering.

Of all my misdeeds, though, none irked my wife so much as my habit of holding my daughter halfway up to the ceiling, to play a semi-improvised game called Baby on the Flying Trapeze. "If you drop her," Sharon would snap, "I will *never* let you touch her for the rest of your life." What I found so provoking, in addition to the sharp tone of voice that immediately turned me into a defiant six-year-old, was the assumption that our game—in which, I might add, Amanda participated eagerly—would inevitably end in bloodshed. For the first time in our lives together, Sharon didn't trust me.

For my own part, I found myself wondering fairly frequently whether these vaguely annoying qualities Sharon was exhibiting had always been there and I'd simply neglected to notice them, or whether they were of more recent vintage. Had she, for example, always been secretly intolerant of my need to be surrounded by newsprint? I've always felt more at home in a room with a ready supply of newspapers and magazines, but only since Amanda's arrival had I become, in Sharon's words, "like a gerbil that needs nesting material."

I suspected, in fact, that it wasn't clutter that Sharon objected to, but *my* clutter. She certainly seemed bent on filling the house with stuff that was theoretically useful but, from a practical standpoint, marginal. "Stuff" is a pretty vague word, I realize, but it's the only one that seems to encompass such diverse gimcracks as a swiveling three-tiered tray for baby food jars, a terry cloth spill protector for Amanda's car seat, a bubble-making windmill with suction cups that adhered to the side of the tub, a multi-compartment travel snack tray, and a zip-up diaper holder that hung from the doorknob of Amanda's closet and would have been quite handy if the closet hadn't been clear on the other side of the room from the changing table.

With our cash flow at a dribble, I couldn't see the logic of shelling out for objects that, as often as not, went unused after a week. After several excruciatingly small-minded arguments—I can't tell you how grateful I am that I've totally erased all of the actual dialogue from my mind—Sharon's penchant for these whatsits became A Subject Not to Be Discussed. And she kept buying them.

Our petty resentments—which we'd always previously managed either to sidestep or to treat with the bemused disrespect they deserved—suddenly assumed front-and-center in our day-to-day conversation. And now nobody had much of a sense of humor. It was gradually becoming clear that both Sharon and I were suffering from separate cases of tunnel vision with a common source: our child. As far as Sharon was concerned, I'd become a distraction, a nuisance. And I was feeling the same about her.

To put this as directly as possible, we now cared about Amanda the way we'd once cared about each other.

Not that we ever attempted to get to the root of the problem. Who had the time or energy for that? Instead we continued our sniping and went to bed in shifts. The irony was that at a time when circumstances were calling on us to work together more closely than ever before, we'd never felt less like partners.

What made our waning patience for each other even more depressing to contemplate was that we both realized we'd been spared probably the single most stressful element of new parenthood: sheer exhaustion. We were habitually tired, sure, but we'd been given a major blessing when Amanda first slept soundly through the night at the age of roughly one week. (She has continued that laudable practice to this very day.) It's truly grisly to contemplate what might have happened to us had middle-of-the-night feedings been added to the menu.

And now we come to the part of the story where, traditionally, I tell you how Sharon and I overcame all our problems and became an upbeat, conflict-free couple. Well, it didn't happen.

I mean, there is a *sort* of happy ending to all this. But it's a real-life happy ending—in other words, it's tentative and ongoing. Our marriage looks to have survived its harrowing detour, and it's now back on a road that we think is leading somewhere we want to go together. But even that statement is a little misleading, because one of the most constructive changes that has come about in our relationship is that we no longer assume that we always want the same things, or that we *need* to always want the same things. Unless, of course, they're the things we want for Amanda.

If this were a work of fiction, I could invent a climactic moment that marked a turning point for us—a scene in which our daughter asks innocently, "Why do you and Mommy always yell at each other?" and the shamed parents resolve to sort out their differences and make a brave new start. Well, for one thing, Amanda can't form sentences of more than two or three words just yet. For another, neither Sharon nor I have ever been much on issuing ultimatums or making reckless promises. We're more inclined to put our faith in everyday behavior.

So what turned us around? I'm still not sure. Somewhere in the seventh or eighth month of parenthood, I noticed that we were muttering less and agreeing more. Perhaps we'd simultaneously reached a point where parenthood was a part we'd played long enough that we could relax a little and devote some serious attention to each other—maybe even start talking and listening honestly again.

Without consciously carving out a block of time, we found ourselves starting to talk over a glass of wine after Amanda had been put to sleep. Before long, we recovered the knack for communicating in the jokey but unsparing way we'd had with each other before parenthood. The reason it happened, I still think, is the simplest possible one: because we wanted it to.

We said a lot of things that no doubt rankled the other. But we agreed on a lot of things, too—most importantly that we were entirely unprepared for what a baby would do to our marriage. When you thought about it, however, what else could we have expected? I guess others had tried to issue discreet warnings (except for my college friend, who had all but rammed the red flag down my throat). But every couple thinks they're different. And they're right. However, it's also true that nearly all of us have our susceptibilities.

Sharon and I agreed that to compare our pre-Amanda re-

lationship to the post-Amanda version would be pointless—
it would be like an astronomer comparing two earthly bod-
ies before and after they'd been pulled into the gravitational
field of Jupiter. As dopey and simplistic as it sounded, our
lives in the present came down to a basic choice: We could
love and enjoy our daughter separately or together. Our mutual ardor for her could become a bond between us or a
wedge.

At the same time, we both came to realize that even
though little remained from what our life as a twosome had
been, who we were had remained more or less intact. In that
way, it was a great stroke of luck that we'd started out as
pals. (You think I'd take a woman to a home-style Pakistani
restaurant to *impress* her?) Even before we'd begun loving
each other, we'd liked each other. And for all our quibbling,
we still did. Maybe it was no longer possible for each of us
to put the other first, but being second wasn't such an un-
palatable alternative.

Finally, we decided that we both needed clearance to en-
tertain and occasionally express murderous thoughts toward
the other, as long as they didn't translate into actual mayhem.

Of course, this is only one couple's story, and a relatively
tame one at that. I wouldn't argue if you judged our marital
difficulties trivial in comparison with the tales of alcoholism,
abandonment, unhinged behavior, and vicious fights about
money or emotional turf that a lot of other couples go
through. Relative to that stuff, our life has been an episode
of *I Love Lucy*.

But in a sense that only reinforces my point: In a baby's

presence, every couple will find the vulnerable spot in their marriage, whatever it may be, and begin to pick at it. If the big issues aren't particularly a problem for you, the small ones will do.

In the long run, the postpartum struggles that Sharon and I have survived (I think) probably did us some good. For all our life together up until Amanda was born, we'd been co-creators of a world that closely resembled the real world in most respects, but had many of the unpleasant parts edited out. For a number of years, the strategy had served us well, but you can only get away with that sort of thing for so long. Having Amanda threw open the windows of a house we hadn't realized was getting stuffy and stale.

Our life now may not be as smooth and pleasant as it once was—it can seem downright menacing at times—but our marriage is immeasurably richer. I see Sharon far more clearly than I ever did before. Her portrait is no longer idealized. In fact, it is sometimes distinctly unflattering, as I'm sure mine is. But the fineness of detail is remarkable, and the subject matter remains spellbinding.

HIGH HOPES

When Amanda was maybe three weeks old, a thought popped into my head as I watched her tiny form curled up in her bassinet, lost in sleep after a day spent grappling with the partly joyful, partly baffling condition called existence that her mother and I had foisted upon her. It was the sort of thought that often comes to men who look into bassinets containing their brand-new daughters and who are beginning to see the world in a totally different way.

Why is it, I wondered, that parents aren't required to make some sort of vow to their newborn children? When two people get married, they are compelled to take part in a ceremony during which they swear that their intentions toward each other are not merely honorable, but glorious. Furthermore, they do this, as a rule, in front of numerous witnesses.

Yet when those two people have a child, the law stipulates little more than that the child's basic physical needs be met. There's nothing on the books that enjoins parents to raise a happy, loved child, or even to put forth an effort to do so. Any good intentions are, I guess, a bonus. As I looked down on our delicate, flawless child with her Cupid's-bow lips, her chestnut hair flecked with gold, her dreamless expression, I reflected once more on how utterly dependent she was on her mother and me—and how lucky she was that her parents depended on her just as completely.

On second thought, I said to myself, wouldn't those vows be utterly superfluous? After all, biology inevitably asserts itself in us once we become parents—we can't help but be blinded by our love for our babies. If the parents of a small child aren't going to act in good faith, who will?

I realized that my greatest fear about Amanda is that despite my every honest attempt to raise her as best I know how, I could well screw it up. I could take this perfect child and somehow ruin her happiness, just because I'd never stopped to think about what exactly I want her to understand and feel about life when she's grown. This is no time to wing it, I said to myself as I looked at my child. You'd better have a plan.

That's how I came to make up what I informally think of as my fatherhood vows. They're really just a list of the things I hope to provide for Amanda, and the things I hope she knows by the time her mother and I are forced to relinquish her to the world.

Interestingly enough, just the effort of putting these vows

together—and the internal inventory I had to take in order to do it—has already made my grip on fatherhood feel firmer. This is a document I plan to reconsult on a regular basis; I've already added to it a few times. And with any kind of luck, it will become even more useful as Amanda grows. If you want to know how things turn out, talk to me in twenty years or so.

Anyway, Amanda, here are my hopes:

I hope you don't grow up thinking you have to be perfect, or that you have to make everybody (and especially your parents) happy all the time. I hope you won't be frustrated by your small failures, and I pray I'll never come down on you about them. Whether the field of endeavor is school or sports or whatever, if I ever fault you for trying hard but not succeeding, you've got my permission to let me have it.

I hope to be the kind of father who can be counted on to laugh at your jokes, even when—no, make that *especially* when—they're the same ones I told my parents as a kid.

I hope I won't become someone you're ashamed to be seen with in public. Remembering the way I was at thirteen, I'd say there's not a chance in hell you'll acknowledge my paternity then. So I won't expect it. However, by the time you've started college (assuming this is something you want to do), I'd hope my place in your life would be recognized.

I hope you like garlic. This is silly, I realize, but it is a superstition of mine that anyone who does is by definition a well-adjusted human being.

I hope to teach you that the term "God-fearing" refers to respect, not terror.

I hope that when you start getting interested in boys, you won't be attracted either to those who idealize you or those who prey on your insecurities. If you are drawn to equality in your relationships, I'll feel I have succeeded.

I hope I not only remember all your birthdays, but always have a pretty good idea of what you want for a present.

I hope you never see me when I've had too much to drink. It's not that I want to appear to you as having no weaknesses (as if there were a prayer of *that* happening). I just don't want you growing up with the idea that lack of self-control is a family trait.

I hope you grow up to be very fond of horses. Not that I care so much myself, but it would make your mother happy.

I hope I never become so preoccupied with what gets you to act the way I want, whatever the long-term effect, that I forget the most important aspect of bringing up a child: an honest, loving, mutually respectful relationship. I'm sure that on occasion, I'll break down and use bribes or threats, but I hope I never make them a way of life.

I hope your mom and I can pass on to you a love of travel. We've been lucky enough to see a fair bit of the world; we've kissed on a beach in Bora Bora, waddled away from several of Paris's better restaurants, and strolled together by the Imperial Palace in Tokyo at cherry blossom time. I hope you have the chance to do similar things and that you don't take the marvels of the world for granted.

I hope I can restrain myself from correcting your pronunciation and grammar, at least until you're in college.

I hope you always find your mother as beautiful and infallible as you do right now, at six months, as I have since I

31

met her. You should be aware that if I were ever forced to take the side of one of you against the other, I would choose her. But I don't know how I'd manage it.

I hope that when you get a little older, you like Clue. I've been looking for a good excuse to play it for nearly twenty years.

I hope that if you're ever in trouble with a teacher—or any nonfamily authority figure, for that matter—you won't neglect to tell me out of certainty that I'll side with the other adult.

I hope I never spoil you, but also that I'm never ungenerous toward you out of a fear of being soft. I hope you'll never see me merely as a source of favors. However, I also hope I'll be able to bring you pleasure without feeling I'm ruining you. I ask for permission in advance to ruin you a little bit.

I hope you're able to run faster than I could when I was a child. Life's no fun when the person who was just tagged It immediately scans the yard looking for you.

I hope I never hit you. No, that's not really a hope—I know I could never do it. If you see me walk away during a moment of anger, you'll know how close I came.

I hope your loot bag is always filled at Halloween and that I'm not too much of a killjoy about letting you enjoy the harvest of your trick-or-treating.

I hope that, faced with either throwing a ball with you outside or watching someone else throw one inside on television, I never forget that the first choice is the better one—although I don't see why you and I couldn't tube out to a good ball game now and then.

I hope that if you ever become boy crazy, you'll have the courtesy to hide it from me.

I hope you'll come to understand the real value of politeness. True, saying please and thank you and holding doors open for people will help them like you. But I hope you'll be considerate of others because your mother and I have taught you to respect them, not because you want anything back.

I hope you never have to wear eyeglasses. I hated mine so passionately. No child should have to be encumbered by them, either physically or socially.

I hope you turn out to be somewhat—but not *too*—sensible about money. Heaven knows it's the one lesson my father never managed to get through to me.

I hope you always remember that it's one thing to differ in opinion with another person, and quite another to stand in judgment of that person.

I hope that, as your adolescence approaches, you don't become impressed with guys based on their athletic prowess. I'd just as soon like your boyfriends, and when I was in high school, I could never stand those guys, and vice versa.

I hope that in following my impulse to protect you from the vulgar aspects of modern life—which, as I become older and stuffier, seem to make up most of modern life—I don't end up protecting you too much. Even if it sometimes means knowing that you're about to make a big mistake.

I hope my heart always swells the way it does now whenever I see you sleeping.

I hope you will appreciate the splendor of a simple, hearty, lovingly prepared meal. However, if I recall correctly,

I stubbornly preferred take-out hamburgers to my mother's accomplished cooking, so I hope I won't be too hard on you if you turn out to be a contrary eater.

I hope that when, inevitably, you break my stereo in the course of testing its mesmerizing array of knobs and switches, I won't get angry at you because you should "know better." I want always to give you the benefit of the doubt.

I hope you never get tired of being coddled and held. As you march forward toward teendom, you will probably at some point become appalled by my attempts to hug you and otherwise demonstrate affection. If you are, too bad. It's not going to stop me.

I hope I'm successful in teaching you what is to me the most crucial lesson a parent can pass on to a child—that no person is automatically better than another. This principle applies to skin color, gender, nationality, political belief, height, weight, religion, and favorite baseball team (though I *do* wonder about Yankees fans . . .). I hope I give you sufficient belief in your own worth that you don't have to put yourself above others in order to know where you are.

I hope your eyes are always as alert and curious and penetrating and honest as they are now.

I hope most of all that someday you will have a baby of your own. Sure, it'd be nice to be a grandfather, but there's an even better reason. It's the only way you will ever possibly be able to understand how fiercely I love you.

THE MIRACLE CHILD

"**D**o you realize that whenever you talk about your daughter, you never say *anything* negative? All I know about her is how funny and pleasant and smart and generous she is. I'm starting to think she isn't human at all, but some kind of celestial being."

His manner was affable, but the guy at the other end of the phone plainly intended to needle me. What really made his observation sting was that he's a *Parents* contributor whom I edit regularly and like enormously, a child development expert (and, I might add, an exemplary father) whose advice to our readers is so gentle and wise that I occasionally wonder how realistic some of his suggestions could be. If a guy like this was calling *me* a Pollyanna—or whoever Pollyanna's male counterpart might be—then there must be some truth to the charge.

It wasn't the first time I'd heard it. My friend Kevin makes a point of regularly and archly inquiring after "the miracle child." A coworker once teased, "You'll have to take a day off after you see Amanda deck some kid for the first time. It's going to *devastate* you."

After a number of critics weighed in with what was essentially the same review, I decided it might be time to step back and spend a moment reflecting on my conduct in the months since Amanda's birth. I did, and concluded that these folks were on to something. Consider this a confession: I am what is referred to, sometimes snidely, as a doting father. Maybe even one of the extreme examples. I become loquacious, to put it mildly, when the topic turns to my daughter, and I have ways of making sure it does.

However, as I was preparing this confession—not, I'm sure, that it comes as any surprise to you—I came to another conclusion: There is absolutely nothing wrong with a father who expounds at length upon the wonders of his progeny. In fact, I believe it's something all fathers *ought* to be doing, early and often, even if our descriptions turn fulsome once in a while.

My own task as a braggart has been simplified by the fact that Amanda provides a regular supply of top-notch material. This was particularly true in her first year, when she started sleeping through the night almost right off the bat and took to nursing effortlessly, while also being considerate enough to wean herself within days of the appearance of her first tooth. Teething problems? Nope. Starting solid food? A piece of cake. The initial stumbling blocks were, to her, hurdles to leap over without even breaking a sweat.

The credit, I quickly add, belonged exclusively to her. Her mother and I were merely bystanders. Forget that twaddle about babies coming into the world characterless blobs, to be molded by their parents into human beings. Amanda was so wholly herself from the moment she emerged from the womb, her instincts for living so sure, that her mother and I knew right away that our best game plan would be to help her when it seemed necessary, teach her whatever she wanted to know, and otherwise get out of the way and enjoy the hell out of her.

We found ourselves especially grateful for a trait Amanda has displayed from birth: a keenly developed sense of delight. She couldn't have been more than a month or so old when we started to notice it. We'd strap her into a little hammock chair on the dining room table; while we ate, our daughter chatted easily and pleasantly with the flower arrangement immediately to her left. Virtually everything that crossed her path—the mobile of cottony clouds that hovered over her bed, the garish cloth monkey someone had sent as a present, even a turkey baster from the kitchen drawer—engrossed her. She'd examine each and every object with glee and care, cooing as she turned it over in her hands.

A little later, when speech arrived, her vocabulary reflected her appetite for practically everything life offered. I could write a hundred pages' worth of stories demonstrating this, but I'll limit myself to a recent episode that has become a personal favorite in my repertoire of Amanda stories. In her high chair one evening just before dinner, she pointed to a bowl of sliced cucumbers sitting on the table, looked pleadingly toward me, and said, "Have it?" I handed her one of the slices; when she put it in her mouth, a look of pure rapture spread over her face. "I *yuv* it!" she nearly shouted.

The high from that moment lasted several days. It didn't even matter when the cucumber I tried to give her the next day elicited total indifference.

Am I lucky to be the father of a child so even-tempered, fun-loving, affectionate, and intelligent? Silly question. Am I luckier than other fathers? I probably won't really know the answer until I become a parent again, but I strongly suspect not.

You probably don't need to be an especially spiritual man to feel, at the moment of your child's birth, that the forces of beauty and mystery and profundity have just collaborated on a production so powerful it absolutely gobsmacks you. In those first enchanted hours and days, it's inconceivable that you could ever stop being amazed and thankful, or that you could falter in your determination to provide your offspring with the most loving childhood in the history of procreation.

The follow-through, however, is always a little tougher. You can try to point to specific incidents as turning points, but it's usually fruitless; over time the emotional edge just seems to wear down to a dullness. A few sleepless nights, a handful of diaper explosions, an argument or two about money with your wife, and fatherhood quietly makes some inexorable, sad transformation from miracle to job.

Even a kid who has been as relatively easy as Amanda presents relentless needs and imposing burdens. She is not, after all, a celestial being, but a human child. She can be try-ing in the way all toddlers are trying, especially over issues pertaining to her independence. If you attempt to remove her raincoat or lug her upstairs for a bath or get her to use a spoon when she's not in the mood, you'll witness a performance worthy of Marlon Brando at his scenery-chewing best. Moreover, Amanda's very capable of torturing the cat moments after she has solemnly sworn off such diversions. Or playing with the remote, no matter how many times in the past she has been told not to. Or escaping her bedroom several times in the course of a single diaper change.

For me, working at *Parents* proved in an odd way to be a disadvantage when it came to coping with my daughter's imperfections. Somehow, I convinced myself that anyone in my position automatically had a second full-time job, as public relations spokesman for parenthood. And complaining would only hurt the cause.

Sure, I adored my daughter. When I leapt on an opportunity to whip out the latest photos, it was always with genuine glee. But there were also times when I wanted desperately to talk about the stuff that troubled me—for example, the afternoon we went to see some friends with a brand-new baby, and Amanda's jealousy put her in a visit-long snit. Or the surprising depth of my irritation when a last-minute milk spill made me miss my usual bus on a day I couldn't afford to be late to work.

Finally, the camel cracked a vertebra. I was grabbing a sandwich with my friend David that day. We usually take turns praising our kids; he's got a frighteningly smart eight-year-old son named Riley. On this particular afternoon, however, I was dangerously close to bottoming out. Sharon and

I had spent most of the previous night trying to comfort Amanda, whose molars, unlike her first teeth, were proving very heavy weather. Feeling about as discouraged and overwhelmed as I'd ever felt, I wasn't what you'd call a really festive lunch partner.

Nonetheless, David was a brick, as he usually is. There are two ways that one gets a reputation as a brick. One is to listen patiently when a friend has a substantial delivery of personal debris to off-load, and the second is to dispense a genuinely comforting response.

David heard me out, then flashed a grin. He said, "It's good to hear you admit you're having trouble. I was wondering when you'd finally break down. I was starting to think, You know, why should this jerk have it any easier than the rest of us? Not that I'd want you to get out of the habit of telling me how cool Amanda is. There aren't too many guys who love talking about their kids as much as I love talking about Riley. I wish more of my friends did it. Then maybe I wouldn't feel like such a dweeb."

He hesitated, as if debating whether to go on. "This is going to sound really pretentious," he finally said, "but I think that to a large extent, parents create their children a second time, after they're born, by the way we talk about them. Just from all the stories I've heard about Amanda, I've got a strong picture of her in my mind. Who knows how accurate it is? You might even be making up the whole thing. But I'll bet she's got a picture of herself in her own mind that's a lot like the one I have. And if she does, I don't think you're ever going to have a problem with her believing in herself."

"You're right," I said, after a pause. "You do sound pretentious." But I also felt he'd struck on something true.

So why is it that we're much more likely to make jocular insults—if not outright complaints—about our children than to profess our unabashed love? Maybe it's our way of venting our resentment at the effort and anguish our children unwittingly put us through. We're exhausted. We've got too much on our plates already. And we have less time than ever to give our kids. I'm usually not one for statistics, but something I saw recently in a newspaper got my attention: Over the past thirty years, the average amount of time parents and children spend together each week has decreased by twelve hours. That's almost two hours a *day*.

When your encounters with your child are so rare and so brief—and when you've got so little energy left for them—you don't want the kid ruining it by being contrary, selfish, demanding, obnoxious, socially embarrassing, insensitive to your needs. In other words, everything a child naturally is. It's so easy to forget that this little bedlamite is also eminently capable of being funny, charming, smart, generous, insightful, and infinitely loving.

The fact is, kids are work. Kids have always been work, and they will always be work. To hold that against them is the height of unfairness. The far wiser course of action, it seems to me, is to stop blaming children for being children and to do our work instead. And to try like hell to let them know as often as we can that we think they're wonderful—and capable of being even more wonderful. It helps if we believe this ourselves.

41

I try not to hang around for long anymore in conversations that consist of sniping at kids. I'd much rather kick back and enjoy listening to dads who honestly relish their kids. Like my friend Dave telling me about the afternoon he was walking with his two-and-a-half-year-old son, Evan, down Fifth Avenue when they saw a red double-decker tourist bus exactly like the Matchbox his mother brought back from her trip to London. "Look, Daddy!" gasped Evan, pointing an astonished finger at the bus. "It's England!"

Even anecdotes without clearly defined punch lines are fine with me, like the one David told me about how when Riley was two, he invented a game David called "That Way." Whenever Riley saw David reading in the living toom, he took David's hand and said, "C'mon, Daddy," then led him to the foyer. Riley then pointed toward the dining room like an explorer leading an expedition and called out, " 'At way!" David asked, "Should we go that way?" Riley replied in the affirmative, took four or five steps, stopped, thought for a moment, then pointed in a different direction and proclaimed, " 'At way!"

That a toddler could have invented such a game strikes me as a minor miracle. But then, when you're a parent, minor miracles are everyday stuff. I am, finally, so thankful for so many things about my daughter—the way she shares graham crackers with the cat, the way she gallops around the room and whinnies like a horse, the way she kisses with her mouth wide open—that if she decides to dump a box of Cheerios on the kitchen floor once in a while, what kind of ingrate am I to complain? If all this makes me a Pollyanna, then bring on the ringlets and rouge.

AN OPEN APOLOGY TO TIPPER GORE

You might recall that old joke about a conservative being a liberal who just got mugged. If that's true, then a cultural conservative is a liberal who just had a baby.

A long and not entirely smooth road has taken me from the way I used to feel about popular culture to the way I do now. Once upon a time, I was the sort of guy who took a certain perverse pride in knowing all the words to the Velvet Underground's "Heroin"—even though a fear of needles and a surplus of common sense prevented me from ever actually trying the drug. And while never having the slightest interest in catching Freddy Krueger's latest cinematic triumph or ordering up the latest wet T-shirt competition on pay per view (well, maybe I was a *little* interested in the wet T-shirts), I didn't consider either one a really serious threat to civilization.

Today, when Sharon and I are channel-surfing and accidentally come across a babes-and-bondage clip on MTV, we exchange a weary, knowing look as we gaze at our daughter frolicking obliviously in her playpen. In unison we say, only half jokingly, "Convent."

The odd thing is, I'm not even a Catholic. What I am now, however, is a father.

Not that I think it's necessary to go as far as my friend Peter. His political credentials may be fastidiously liberal, but you'd have never guessed it to hear him grilling a mutual friend at lunch not long ago. The topic was a new romantic comedy movie our friend had just seen, and Peter wanted to know whether it would be appropriate to take his ten-year-old son.

"Is there any sex in it?" Peter asked in his best cut-to-the-chase manner.

"Well, not actual sex, no," our friend answered. "But a certain amount of bedroom activity is implied."

Peter turned this somewhat vague information over in his mind for a few seconds. "Okay, then," he continued, "is the word *sex* mentioned?"

"Yes," said the friend definitively. "They do use the word."

Peter waved his hand in a way that indicated the conversation was over. "We're not going," he said.

Although I share Peter's zeal only to a point, I share it enough that I now feel compelled to offer Tipper Gore a sincere apology for the things I used to say about her. Somehow I suspect the news of my disapproval never quite reached her, limited as it was to the ears of my mother and a few close friends, none of whom are equipped with Beltway clout. Still, it never hurts to apologize when you've been unfair.

A few years ago, when she began her crusade against rock lyrics that glorified all those sordid things that Americans can't get enough of, I was among those who were pretty offended by Tipper Gore's stand. Not that I championed the lofty artistic ambitions of Judas Priest or 2 Live Crew or any of the others whom—or so it appeared—she was trying to suppress. The actual songs seemed little more than trivial, witless pieces of adolescent naughtiness designed to get the attention of grown-ups. Hardly worth taking seriously, let alone censoring.

And even if they were, who would define what constituted objectionable material? Were we to trust that government officials—probably the same ones who, not so long ago, designated *The Flintstones* as educational TV—would make the proper distinction between the breathtaking imbecility and squalor of, say, the average Billy Idol video and the unsparing but deadly accurate satire of our debased mass culture that is *The Simpsons?*

And then there was Tipper herself. She had the aura about her of the compulsive do-gooder, the former Pep Club president who'd decided to apply the same dogged energy to getting labels slapped on violent and sexually explicit recordings that she might once have used in an effort to boost school spirit.

Hers was not a stance that appealed to many of us whose view of society was shaped in the crucible of the sixties. I

45

can hardly claim to have a place on the counterculture's cutting edge—I couldn't even stay awake for more than about five minutes of "In-A-Gadda-Da-Vida"—but I did manage to retain at least one earmark of that hippie-touched generation: a highly skeptical attitude toward those who deal in social absolutes, especially when the views held were more conservative than my own.

Then Sharon became pregnant.

As our bringing a child into the world edged toward reality, it was suddenly time to take a harder look at the world into which this child would be brought. I quickly found that my highly principled disdain for censorship was being shoved aside by some very strong practical doubts.

Now, when TV ads for Hollywood's latest idiotically gory slasherfest aired on prime time, they no longer struck me as benign. The vintage *Playboys* that got me through some lean years in college went onto the recycling pile. I started flipping through my album collection, mentally separating them into two piles: records our as-yet-unborn child would be allowed to hear (Aretha Franklin, Buddy Holly) and ones that were off-limits (The Doors, Funkadelic).

I was resolved that our child would never become a slave to popular culture's trashy deceptions. I felt even stronger about it when we found out that our baby would be a girl. It's admittedly Neanderthal of me, but I've noticed in other fathers, too, that our impulse to protect our children from danger takes on added urgency when that child is a girl. Probably it's nothing more than our misguided sense that boys are better able to take care of themselves—in addition to the illogical and highly sexist notion that girls should be as sheltered as boys are experienced.

But it soon dawned on me that my budding enthusiasm for censorship wasn't merely based on some highly questionable assumptions about gender. It was also more than a little hypocritical. What gave me the right to deny my daughter—who wasn't even born yet, for God's sake—her dalliance with the sort of innocent decadence that no kid of a certain age can resist? It wasn't as if I'd skipped any of the major rites de passage when my number had come up.

Finally, I decided, what was turning me into a bluenose was only my fear that innocent decadence maybe isn't so innocent anymore.

I'm hardly the first person to have noted this, but kids today clearly learn about adult things much sooner in their lives than we ever did. So much so, perhaps, that their knowledge often seems to outpace their ability to understand what it is they're learning. Even as gradually as our generation was introduced to the ambiguities and vices of the post-childhood world, it was a struggle to make sense of it all.

Take sex. The truth is, my first brush with soft-core porn was a profoundly unsettling experience, though I would have died rather than admit it to my friends at the time. My initiation came at an eighth-grade sleepover; a bunch of us, cocooned in sleeping bags in Matt Pflieger's basement, took turns reading aloud from someone's older brother's well-thumbed copy of that literary masterwork *Triangle of Lust*.

The plot, as I recall, centered around the female protago-

nist's insatiable desire for . . . well, you know. The spine had
been conveniently pre-cracked, so that when it was your
turn to read, all you had to do was lightly flip the pages until a juicy scene opened up in front of you. This didn't exactly promote the story's chronological flow. Neither did the
preadolescent asides—the laughing and boasting and drool-
ing—that regularly interrupted the reading.

The communal experience of *Triangle of Lust* was nothing
less than intoxicating, but when we finally settled down to
sleep that night, I found my head reeling with disturbing
concepts totally incompatible with the world I knew. Women
wanted men for sex? There were actually grown-ups whose
entire reason for living was what *Triangle of Lust* called—in
an atypically coy but characteristically inaccurate phrase—
"the love act"?

If these notions struck a thirteen-year-old as incomprehensible a couple of decades ago, imagine what it must be
like for today's nine-year-olds to grasp the idea of a condom.
It's hardly any wonder that kids get so confused and bristly
about sex. They couldn't possibly want to know as much
about the subject as the world—in other words, us grown-
ups—forces them to learn.

The same goes for violence, but double. At least there *is*
such a thing as healthy sexuality. It seems pointless here to
take up space arguing against violent entertainment. (Now
there's an oxymoron for you.) It's ultimately what arguing
against Hitler must have been like back in the thirties.
They're both such easy marks, and the protesting does just
as much good.

But what *does* do any good? Not the hard line, that's for sure. It's tempting to shut our eyes and envision a world without sitcom laugh tracks that erupt into hysteria every time a kid says the word *butt,* a world without Megadeth videos, a world without Andrew Dice Clay. But this airbrushed universe will never exist, no matter how fervently vigilante committees and drunk-on-brimstone ministers desire it to be. We've got to deal with a warts-and-all world that seems sometimes to be, in fact, mostly warts. It's a daunting job. As my mother recently told me, "I'm glad I raised you when I did, and not now. I don't think I could keep a child out of trouble today."

I've concluded, for now, that the key to keeping my daughter "out of trouble" is not by waging a full-tilt one-man war on mass culture. All you do is fertilize the ground from which the forbidden fruit springs. But what I *can* do is at least try to render what I consider the bad stuff irrelevant to Amanda's life. My plan, if you can call it that, is based on the assumption that finally, sex, violence, and moral illiteracy in mass media aren't really about sex, violence, or moral illiteracy at all. They're about the one thing children want most of all: power. Or at least a particularly bleak and cynical vision of power, one that comes from bending others to your will, shouting down people who don't believe as you do, and getting your revenge on everyone who ever hurt or insulted you.

What I hope to do is give my daughter a better working definition of power. I hope to teach her that power is understanding what her gifts are and having the confidence to make the most of them without squashing other people and their aspirations. Needless to say, I'm virtually devoid of specifics when it comes to how I propose to convey these lessons. On the other hand, if I really knew how to do it, I'd be God—and I don't mean that figuratively, either.

For the time being, my mother's common-sense rule seems to work well here: The only way you ever teach a child your beliefs is by living them. Like it or not, we all end up being examples. We might as well try to be good ones.

Sharon and I have spent many spouse-hours wrestling with the question of how much to control what Amanda sees and hears. Our solution—at least for now—is to think about the matter in terms of what we're exposing her to, not what we're keeping her from.

Not that we're going to turn into one of those icky couples who force-feed their children Bach fugues and morally uplifting bedtime stories. But we do assume that Amanda will ultimately learn more about how men and women relate to each other by watching us than by watching *Married with Children*. We're hoping that if she's exposed to the music and books, the humor and ideas that we value, there's a chance that she'll learn to value them too. I'm enough of an optimist to believe that if you give a child a choice between diamonds and junk, the child will spurn the junk. (Unless, of course, the junk is My Little Pony or Rainbow Brite.)

Having actually gone back and reread what Tipper Gore said at the time, I now see that when she asked that warning labels be used on certain records, she was getting at much the same point: We don't need to outlaw sexual or violent content, we just need to know where it's found so that we can avoid it, or at least talk to our kids about it. The point of these labels has never been to ban "adult" speech, just to keep it in the world of adults. Who really wants children to have to grapple with the mire of exploitation and abuse— drug abuse, sexual abuse, racial abuse, verbal abuse—that grown-ups have created until the point in their lives when it becomes absolutely necessary?

Before she is grown, Amanda will be tempted by decadence. Unless I miss my guess, it will happen at just about the time she starts to believe that the most reasonable opinions in the world are those voiced by anyone other than her parents. I am resigned to her going through this stage; after all, why should she be any different from her father and mother? I just hope that at some point she'll see what she stands to lose by being jaded, and that she understands the bargain is a lousy one.

It's so easy to fall into despair about the world that faces our children. I have sometimes wondered whether there was even a point in trying to preserve Amanda's innocence. Then, recently, something happened that gave me a degree of hope.

We were at a family resort that had one of those karaoke sing-along setups. One afternoon I happened to be passing by as a group of school-age girls, all looking to be between seven and nine, stood in line waiting to sing the pop songs of their choice. I sat down to listen.

The first girl launched into a painfully flat but self-assured version of Madonna's "Material Girl." Listening to a child who'd barely gotten rid of her baby teeth coyly purring, "Little boys who save their pennies make my rainy day," was more or less heartbreaking. The second girl, also a Madonna fan, opted for that quaint mishmash of religious and erotic imagery, "Like a Prayer." The fact that neither of these girls could possibly have any idea what the words really meant provided little comfort.

Then came the third girl, tall and ponytailed and more than a little gawky. The karaoke machine played the introduction to a slow song that I could almost, but not quite, place. Then she started to sing, in a soft, tuneless, but nonetheless heartfelt voice: "Somewhere over the rainbow, bluebirds fly. . . ." Her eyes were closed, her hands held the microphone tightly. I rose abruptly from the table and started walking briskly toward the exit, at the same time attempting to jog loose the lump that had instantly formed in my throat. She was still singing as I left the room. "If bluebirds fly, then why, oh why, can't I?"

I never saw her again. However, I think about that girl surprisingly often. I hope she grows up okay, that the other kids don't tease her for being a dweeb, that she doesn't believe them if they do, and that she grows up to find a life filled with tenderness and hope and passion. After all, Sharon and I owe her a lot. For one thing, "Over the Rainbow" is now Amanda's official lullaby.

HOME AT LAST

For a couple that has always lived a rung or two up from genteel poverty, Sharon and I have grabbed our fair share of high living. The jobs we had during our courtship and early married years allowed us to spend time in what seemed like the best possible way, roaming the world and chowing down magnificently wherever we happened to find ourselves. At the same time, we pulled in so little money that worrying about it didn't make much sense. This was true of my work especially; I was writing a lot for travel magazines, an occupation that combines intensely glamorous working conditions with a pay scale just this side of a ditchdigger's.

"So you must really feel your style is cramped," several people said, directly or obliquely, right after Amanda was born. "You used to really get around. Now you're stuck at home with a baby." For some reason they directed the question to me, not Sharon, and I got the feeling they'd be asking it even if I hadn't had such a freewheeling, globe-trotting pre-fatherhood life. After all, every man is supposed to feel the walls closing in from the moment the baby comes home from the hospital, right?

Well, actually, no. It would crush some men I know to admit this, but because fatherhood has stripped me of every shred of pride, I may as well tell the world: I'd rather be at home than anywhere I can think of. Travel—both literally and metaphorically—is no longer my preferred means of escape.

Not that I've become totally immune to the virus. On certain slushy mid-February days, my mind meanders back to previous journeys, and it's hard to avoid thinking about, say, an outdoor table at Sufferers Jerk Pork & Chicken Centre on Boston Bay, up on the north coast of Jamaica. Similarly, a certain Paco de Lucia record awakens in me the desire for a stroll through central Madrid and a *mojito* at Chicote, where the bartenders dress like funeral home directors and mix cocktails that possess mystical powers. At other moments I get the urge to drive a mountain pass in the Swiss Alps or listen to Mexican bands play jury-rigged *rancheros* in a dusty marketplace in San Antonio or warm a stool at a Connemara pub listening to the local fishermen mutter to each other in Gaelic.

But these notions aren't really trying to seduce me. They're only flirting. And besides, whenever I picture myself anywhere else in the world, it's never without the rest of the family in tow. (Except in the bars, of course.)

The pathetic truth is this: My only solo travel since our daughter's birth was a three-day business trip to San Francisco—arguably the most idyllic city in America, the place virtually all of us would choose as home if we could only find any damned jobs there. To characterize this visit as "miserable" taxes to the limit my powers of understatement.

I had heard friends speak of toddler withdrawal, but until that trip I never knew its ravages. By the middle of the second afternoon, for me to see a small child on the street hand in hand with a parent was like being introduced to an electrified fence. And, of course, every toddler in northern California made a point of placing herself directly in my line of vision. It got so bad that, when I caught the eye of an especially winsome two-year-old in a floral frock that would make Amanda a heartbreaker on an off-day, only an awareness of the legal ramifications kept me from sweeping this tiny stranger into my arms and planting numerous smooches on her cheeks.

Still, happily rooted to the hearth though I am, it would be more than a little dishonest for me not to admit that on the day our daughter came home from the hospital, I had some second thoughts about the liberties I'd just surrendered.

That day was a Sunday, so the world was a little quieter than usual to begin with. My mother had just left the house; Sharon's was about to arrive. Sharon and Amanda were upstairs nursing as I sat in the living room having a discreet—and, as far as I am concerned, perfectly legitimate—panic attack.

No doubt contributing to my mental state was the fact that I had been up for three-quarters of the night before, uttering my child's name over and over, fashioning the story of her birth into a narrative I could recite to her in years to come. As I lay sleepless, I recalled her face—tomato-red and inexpressibly dear—in those first few hours, and tried to imagine what her life was going to be like. For the past thirty-six hours, I now realized, I had been devoting practically every waking moment to totting up the things that Amanda would add to our lives. It suddenly became clear that some subtracting would be necessary, too.

In large part, I'd started looking forward to becoming a father when the pleasures that had for Sharon and me—as for so many dual-income, no-tomorrow couples—comprised the good life began to seem a mite puny and pointless. It had gradually dawned on both of us that there had to be more satisfying, profound things to do with our lives.

So now Amanda was here, and I'd gotten the heightened sense of meaning I wanted from life. And all I could think of was: No travel. No eating in restaurants. No going to movies. No listening to jazz in clubs. No disposable income. No fun. It seemed worse than unfair. It seemed like some sort of royal retribution for a life of brazenly misspent yuppiness.

At dinner that night, I said to Sharon, "It's not that I don't love Amanda to pieces. And I would gladly stop an oncoming bus with my bare hands and wrestle it to the ground for her. But all this . . . I mean . . ." I paused from my babbling to take a mouthful of her mother's meltingly tender fried chicken, which for some reason turned to powder the moment it entered my mouth. "I know this is juvenile, but part of me wants to get on an airplane right now and just *go* somewhere."

Annoyingly calm, my wife gave this a few moments' thought, then did something unexpected. She started laughing. "I have to say, the thought of running away crossed my mind once or twice," she finally said. "Not seriously, of course. I *was* thinking, though, that if having her around is a big change for us, just think of how much things have changed for her. There she was, nice and snug and happy inside her mother, and now she finds herself"—she made a vague circle with her hand to indicate the entire world in its protean oddness—"in *this* place."

As she so often does, Sharon had stepped in and with a single, almost offhand observation, restored perspective. It was several days before I absorbed the full import of her words, it embarrasses me to say. But in the days that followed, I found myself imagining Amanda's reactions to all the new stuff she was seeing and hearing and taking in; when I looked into her amazed eyes, whatever sense I had of being overwhelmed seemed piffling. And the more I tuned in to her, the less inclined I was to keep an eye on the exit doors.

During that first week, as Amanda groped her way toward a sleep routine, I made a heartening discovery: Nothing did quite as tidy a job of restoring her to unconsciousness when she awoke howling at three A.M. as playing her one of my Tito Puente records as I swayed her to and fro. Ten minutes of those relentless Latin rhythms and she was a dishrag. Thus it occurred to me that my daughter and I could combine our pleasures—which became one more reason for spending every free moment of my life with her.

As she's gotten older, this has gotten even easier. She's not quite ready for Pink Panther movies or Thai food—not yet, anyway—but she adores one of my culinary specialties, escarole sautéed in olive oil with a little garlic. And she seems to enjoy having me read nineteenth-century novels aloud to her as she's winding down to sleep. Trust me, I'm not doing this for her sake; I figure it's the only way I'll ever be disciplined enough to get through *Crime and Punishment*. It's obvious she doesn't understand a word I'm reading, but the rhythm of the language sends her effortlessly into the arms of the Sandman, so things work out for everybody.

In the meantime, as she gets older and her personality begins to emerge, Amanda's unfolding story has actually come to resemble a good nineteenth-century novel; it takes a few slow chapters before things get rolling, but soon you're reading as fast as you can to get to the next scene. Each evening brings the latest installment in the serial of my daughter's life. The key scene tonight might be a stirring journey through her alphabet book, or a bitterly disappointing dinner that includes carrots. You never know just what twists this plot is going to take.

That's probably why I concern myself so seldom anymore with ducking out of our domestic life. Enjoying it takes up pretty much all my time.

The one thing I do miss is frequent contact with guy friends. We still grab lunches on a regular enough basis and occasionally squander our companies' time and telephone budgets catching up, just like in the old days. But it's more occasional now. I miss the couple of nights per month when I used to grab a couple of buddies after work and let the beer and bonhomie take over for a couple of hours. I miss being up-to-date about my unmarried friends' labyrinthine romantic lives, hearing the same raunchy jokes everybody else heard first, and dissecting in infinite detail recent Mets games (although this last exercise has gotten rather painful over the past few years).

But most of all I miss my softball team. It hardly matters that my exile is self-imposed. Sharon has been generous about trying to nudge me back onto the field, but on the few occasions that I have donned the hallowed blue and gold of the Consenting Adults (that's the team's name, honest) and taken my station at first base, my mind has had a way of drifting mid-inning to other things. Like the way my daughter pushes me over when I'm sitting cross-legged on the carpet, then tumbles into my arms as I fall. Or her chestnut curls. Or her cornflower blue eyes. Once I found out that by skipping the postgame revels I could make it home in time to put her to bed, McAleer's Pub didn't have a prayer. And once I gave up McAleer's, the game itself seemed an afterthought.

I didn't fully realize how much my life had changed until recently, when the three of us spent the day with Rick and Monica, a so-far-childless couple we've known for a long time. Both having stuck with the line of work I abandoned, they continue to hew a robust path through the world, enjoying a way of life we're not even close to being able to afford anymore, financially or emotionally.

That afternoon marked the first time either Rick or Mon-

ica had laid eyes on Amanda, and both were paying a reasonably embarrassing amount of attention to her as she in-
vestigated the dandelions in their yard, drove her Big Bird
bus all over their picnic table, and periodically ran to us for
reassurance. They were obviously making mental notes on
the way we talked to her and smooched with her and sang
along with the Bonnie Raitt album as we swung her around
the patio. As lovely and relaxing as that afternoon was,
Sharon and I couldn't help but feel those two relentless sets
of eyes. It was as if we were the subjects of somebody's an-
thropology thesis.

Over Rick's *fusilli al tonno,* we heard about his and Monica's recent assaults on Sweden (we were mildly curious),
the west of Ireland (periodic sighs of nostalgia), and Gas-
cony (major salivating during Monica's foie gras-buying
story). And then Rick said, maybe not quite as casually as he
intended to, "Don't you miss it?" He was nominally address-
ing both Sharon and me, but as usual I felt the weight of the
question intended for my shoulders.

There was a moment of awkwardness. "Not at all," Sharon
said offhandedly. "It was great when we were doing it, but I
got a little traveled out toward the end."

It took a little longer for me to answer. "To tell you the
truth, there *are* a few things about my old life that I miss.
There are a lot more I totally forgot about the moment I became a father. But when it comes to travel, Amanda's brain
is by far the most exotic destination I have ever visited. And
it's a good thing, too, because we didn't exactly get round-
trip tickets."

Just at that moment, there was a howl from the corner of the patio. Amanda had scraped her knee on the flagstones and was stumbling toward us, blubbering and streaming tears. "Remind me," I murmured to our hosts as I folded my girl in my arms, "to give her a little help with her timing."

BREADWINNING WITHOUT LOSING

Shortly before Amanda was born, Sharon and I made a bilateral decision that, in this day and age, might be considered peculiar. Several people we know have praised our alleged exercise in good sense, while others have discreetly twitted us for our social backwardness. We weren't looking to make a statement of any sort; we simply felt our daughter should have one parent on duty full-time for at least her first few years. And because my paycheck was marginally more likely to support all three of us, and because I've generally enjoyed working more than Sharon has, it seemed logical that I'd be the one to remain in the labor force.

This arrangement makes us, I guess, the sort of typical family that's not so typical anymore.

As I say, our decision has not met with unanimous applause among our acquaintances. Specifically, Sharon has taken flak in some quarters over "settling" for housewifery. But the fact of the matter is, she is a superb mother who puts as much energy and care and intelligence into the job of making Amanda a happy, curious, well-adjusted child as any of our women friends who are executives plow into their work. And quite honestly, as long as what she's doing brings her satisfaction, I don't care where my wife puts her efforts.

When it comes to my own work situation, I'm luckier than a lot of guys; in many ways, *Parents* is the model of a pro-dad office. When Sharon gave birth, I was all but shoved out the door, with pay, for the first weeks of my daughter's life. (This in a society where men frequently have to cash in their vacations just so they can hang out with their newborns.) I also work in one of the few offices I know where putting in ridiculous hours is not part of the unwritten loyalty test and where a man can get a day off if his child has a medical emergency—no questions asked, no eyebrows raised, someone will cover for you. And *no* one says offhandedly, "Can't your wife take care of that?"

Even better, my coworkers do better than humor me— they often express actual interest in my highly detailed updates on Amanda's life. (With plentiful visual supplements, of course.)

Nonetheless, even under the best of conditions, I've found that this curious new title, primary wage earner, takes some adjustment. For those of us who hold this title, there's a lot not to love.

For example, take the periodic panic attacks caused by the

sudden thought that your life is turning out exactly like your father's. The only way I've been able to maintain a clear distance is to keep reminding myself that Dad never understood what was so terrible about Spiro Agnew.

But this particular anxiety hides a deeper one, I think, and one that's more legitimate: the sense that from now on, your life is to be dictated by duty, not pleasure. When you feel your primary purpose in life is to cough up a paycheck, it's but a short step to the conviction that you're getting a crummy deal. And once you accept that proposition, your days start to take on the characteristics of a wine that has turned. To avoid this trap, I'm doing my utmost to view breadwinning as an offering I make to my family out of gratitude for their presence in my life, not as opening a vein because somebody else has a claim on a percentage of my blood.

If you're like most new dads, you've also put in a fair chunk of time weighing your chances of getting your financial house even remotely in order. Consequently, you nurse bitter thoughts. My friend Mark perfectly summed up the attitude of a lot of us when he once asked, "Did you notice that when your child is born, money simultaneously becomes the least important thing in the world and the most important thing in the world?"

Yes, I *did* happen to notice that, Mark. I've also noticed the number on my pay stub, and it started looking a lot less impressive when it represented our household's total income for the month.

Of course, discretionary income is little more than a memory to us now. But in the end, Sharon and I have decided, who really gives a flying Filofax? Not that either of us would ever have made anybody's honor roll of conspicuous consumers, but nowadays I can honestly claim total indifference to the thought of shelling out for a Range Rover or an Armani suit. (Anyway, I once tried on an off-white Italian-cut double-breasted job just out of curiosity. I looked like one of those icing bags that bakers squeeze when they're writing people's names on cakes.)

For me, the most noxious reality of all, which I face five times weekly, is catching a commuter bus each morning at eight A.M. and returning almost twelve hours later. This gives me a little less than an hour with my daughter after she wakes, and another hour and a half or so before she goes to bed. It's hardly a wonder that I sometimes get the feeling so familiar to new fathers: that we end up putting so much effort into keeping our families financially afloat that we don't have much of a chance to get to know them.

That's probably why I so often find myself slipping into envy when I consider the lot of stay-at-home dads. I know a few, and they're always so disarmingly content, with this cat-that-ate-the-canary attitude that's not quite smugness but can get pretty close. Of course, many of these men also talk about how isolated they feel, how little respect they get from their peers, how their natural comrades—the women who are also full-time parents—frequently view them with profound distrust, if not open hostility. In my less charitable moments, knowing these men's lives are less than ideal is something of a solace.

Not precisely the most becoming reaction, I'll admit. But it's easy to become resentful when you feel this persistent, urgent need to satisfy not only your bosses but your family, and then maybe yourself. At the worst times, a man's life can seem to boil down to one big, ugly question: Do I want to be a failure as a wage earner or as a parent?

However, before we breadwinners all resign ourselves to chumphood, let's take a moment to get some perspective. Perhaps we could start by being grateful we even realize that dissatisfaction is an option. To many dads of the previous generation, the very idea that you could *be* an involved father while holding down a job was sort of like suggesting that a guy could pay thirty dollars for a haircut and still be heterosexual. A very gung ho new dad I know once said, a little self-righteously, "I can't understand why it never bothered my father that he hardly knew us. He acted as though he couldn't possibly have had anything in common with us, especially when it came to any sort of an emotional bond."

The old man might indeed have been a jerk, but for the moment let's resist the urge to father-bash. (Among other things, the karmic consequences are unbecoming.) It just could be that this guy's problem wasn't a lack of feeling for his children, but a sense that tenderness, caring, and being part of their lives simply weren't part of the job description. Unless, of course, the involvement centered around something unassailably masculine and emotionally neutral—playing catch, say.

The difference between then and now was brought home to me the day after Amanda was born. I was driving my mother to the hospital to visit her granddaughter for the first time. I told Mom all about the delivery and what it was like to actually see my daughter enter the world. I finished the story by saying, "All I could think of afterward is how Dad, and every guy in his generation, really got cheated by not being around for their kids' births."

Mom smiled ruefully. I gathered from this that she might have liked the father of her child in the delivery room, but she simply said, "Well, that wasn't the way things happened then. Men were just made to feel they didn't belong there. It's hard to understand why now, but it seemed to make sense at the time."

The more I thought about her response, the more I suspected that my dad had missed out on even more than I'd originally thought. When you're not considered important enough to be present at the beginning of your child's life— when, in fact, you're considered a mild headcase if you *want* to be—then at what point of that life do you start feeling important? No wonder it was so hard sometimes for our fathers to feel attached to us.

But if the curse that dogged men of the previous generation was the limited role they were relegated to, our burden is the breadth of choice we've been given, in combination with the oppression we often feel about choosing the wrong thing—say, career over family. Or maybe it's vice versa.

How is each of us supposed to make his way through this minefield of obligations? In search of answers, I've spent a fair bit of time talking to some dads I know who seem to have resolved the conflict—or at least hammered out a nonaggression pact—between their home and work lives. I offer these suggestions not with the expectation that you will be struck dumb by their dazzling ingenuity. What's truly surprising about the stratagems we often use to successfully get through life is that they are so utterly unoriginal and commonsensical.

Rule One is by far the most crucial one, and it remains constant among virtually all the dads I know: Make peace with your life's boundaries, and keep remembering how lucky you are. We can all find grounds for dissatisfaction with our jobs, our families, or both. However, most of us have at least one reason to be profoundly grateful: We have children. And in the final analysis, we love them, they love us, and we all know it.

An older father I know once delivered a cocktail-party soliloquy that contained some of the wisest and most gracious things I ever heard anyone say about children. I remember it almost word for word. "I've always thought my kids were so wonderful that no sacrifice I could make for them ever *seemed* like a sacrifice," he said. "And the thing about it is, they've really never asked much of me that I was unwilling to give.

"Most of the time, when parents complain to their children about this or that—you must think I'm made of money, or you don't appreciate how hard I work so that you can blow it on a pair of hundred-dollar sneakers—I think kids see that as the parent giving them reasons for wishing they hadn't *become* parents. So often these are the kids who make the greatest demands. I figure what they're really asking for is a commitment, proof they really *matter* to their parents. Kids really don't want material things from us as much as we think they do."

These words, I find, give me pause every time my role as provider tempts me to feel sorry for myself.

But another, even more unseemly problem arises when fathers complain about our lives: We become far more boring people. As my friend David says, "Martyrs never get invited to the really great parties." Probably even more than Sharon, Amanda doesn't want to hear about the tie-up outside the Lincoln Tunnel that delayed the bus for a half hour, or how many stories I've got to have edited by the end of the week. And they're entitled to feel that way. Listening to me bellyache is not in my daughter's contract—not for another few years, anyway.

We fathers just have to come to terms with the intractable reality that having a job, having a family, and caring about both means that you've got to work within certain limitations. If they seem unreasonable, you do just as you would when faced with anything else that's unreasonable in your life: You make the necessary changes. And if you're smart, you put your family's desires first.

Does this formula oversimplify a lot of difficult situations? Sure it does. But when we're under too much pressure, we humans have a way of overcomplicating matters and coming up with all sorts of perfectly sound reasons to remain in the same miserable predicament. Sometimes thinking simply is the only way to unravel the knot.

Just as basic as Rule One, yet similarly elusive, is Rule Two: When you're working, make sure you're truly working, and when you're with your children, try to make sure you're truly with your children. Wayne, a friend of mine whose kids are both in school, revealed his gimmick for cleansing the workday from his brain. "Every day, when I pull the car into the driveway, I turn off the ignition key, take a deep breath, and say to myself, 'Your bosses won't remember you in twenty years, but your kids will.' Then I go inside, and I feel as if I've just started the day all over again. It sounds a little New Agey, maybe, but it works."

My own method of carrying out Rule Two is profoundly uncreative, but effective: I make sure I'm the first person my daughter sees in the morning and the last one she sees at night. When Amanda calls for her milk at seven A.M. or so, I pluck her from the crib, change her, and take her downstairs for a nice fresh bottle. We then chat and play, or maybe snuggle on the couch and watch a Madeline video for a while, until I transfer her to her mother so that I can pull myself together for work. In the evening, from the moment I set foot in the house, I belong to Amanda. Her agenda becomes mine. At bedtime, it is my duty and pleasure to pajama her and present the good-night bottle before laying her down.

This arrangement works nicely for everyone. Amanda can depend on her day starting and ending in a consistent, pleasant way. Sharon gets a break from a child who, while delightful, tends to go at life hammer and tongs. And me? I not only get to spend time with the most delectable little girl ever born, but also to feel I'm an essential part of her daily life.

A few dads I've talked to extol the virtues of devoting an occasional day off to hanging out with their kids. "To me, it's an extension of the mental health days I used to take a couple of times a year before we became parents," said one dad who wishes to remain anonymous in case his boss is reading this. He adds, "I always make sure that whenever I take off a daddy day, my wife has somewhere else to go. She just gets in the way of our fun."

Considering that back when we were teenagers together, his idea of fun included putting Limburger in the school's ventilation system, I think his wife has every reason to want to stick around. However, she's gracious enough to bow out. I think she knows how important these little furloughs are to his sanity.

Along those lines, Rule Three is: Try not to look at the time you spend with your kids as a claim on your energy. Granted, sometimes it *is*. Maybe a lot of the time. And when that's the case with me, I feel justified in seeking adult assistance—spousal or otherwise—so I can at least catch my breath. But sometimes, at those times when I'm not dealing with the work-family thing particularly well, the problem is one of perspective.

I have to confess that sometimes it's exhausting even to contemplate a spirited game of ring-around-the-rosy immediately upon returning home, as is the current custom in our home. (Sometimes I am permitted to change into civvies, sometimes not.) In theory, diving into strenuous activity with a child places an added burden on a nervous system that feels perilously close to overload. However, in practice, odd as it sounds, when I hold my daughter's hands and we skip in a circle, then fall on our bums at the (more or less) simultaneous moment, the effect on me is a near-total physical and emotional recharge. The aftertaste of the workday vanishes. Of course, the wicked giggle that she breaks into as her behind hits the floor helps a lot.

Amanda's a little young for Rule Four to have relevance. But when the time comes in a few years, I'll be ready. It is: Teach your children to accept the fact that you have to work.

Kids don't automatically see the link between the time you spend away from home and the roof that keeps the rain from falling on their heads. Natural egoists that they are, they're incapable of grasping the importance of anything that keeps you away from them. You have two choices here. You can lead them to believe that work is a punishment for the crime of adulthood (and even if you're adolescent enough to believe this is true, do you really want your kids to have the same attitude?). Or you can help them understand work as an intermittently frustrating but necessary, potentially fulfilling, maybe even important part of life.

My friend Jack, whose son is six, says, "When I leave for the office in the morning, I tell Jay I'll be thinking about him all through the day, and it'll be great to see him when I get home. But I *never* tell him that I'll be sad, or that I'll miss him. To me, all that says to him is that I'd rather not be working, but that I do it for his sake. That's a lot of guilt to hang on a kid. Besides, he doesn't need to develop the attitude that work is a bad thing."

And Wayne told me that when his five-year-old daughter suddenly became very curious as to why her friends' daddies and sometimes their mommies had to work, he explained matters to her as best he could and crossed his fingers that she'd get it. She must have, because soon afterward she asked a grown-up family friend about his job, adding, "Kindergarten is *my* job."

Which brings us to Rule Five, possibly the most important rule of all, especially if your wife works too: Do your best not to backslide into the fifties.

This is in many ways the hardest promise to keep, as most of us know from personal experience. By now I think most men are sufficiently evolved to understand that for a wife to maintain a home and raise children requires as much effort— and deserves as much respect—as toiling in an office. However, it's one thing to grasp that fact, and another to truly absorb it. Sheepishly, I concede that I sometimes need to be reminded that Sharon's plate is just as full as mine is.

The strange thing is, the times when I tend to need prodding on this matter come not so much when I'm tired and disheartened, but when I've come home feeling self-satisfied. *That's* when I'm liable to tell myself, "You've damn well done enough for one day. Just pull on your jeans, pop a cold one, and tube out for a couple of hours. You've earned it."

Nice thought, but obviously what I've earned or haven't earned isn't at issue here; when you get right down to it, all of us who manage to keep either a career or a family afloat—never mind both of them—deserve at the very least a month on a tropical beach, starting tomorrow. But I somehow doubt we'll be seeing each other on the plane down.

If there's one complaint I hear most often from mothers today, it's that husbands who are admirably engaged with their kids—who gladly change diapers or take the baby out on errands so that Mom can catch a breather—still don't even dream of taking on the real grunt work of parenthood. This beef is, to a large degree, justified. Fathers probably ought to be more hands-on when it comes to dealing with the pediatrician or investigating preschools or keeping their children's closets organized.

But while it's up to us to do better, it's also up to our wives to understand that our progress—and never forget that we *have* made substantial progress—sometimes feels unnatural. We didn't grow up playing with dolls. We weren't prepared for an adulthood that included this sort of responsibility, as girls were. Our dads by and large gave household matters a wide berth, and we were indirectly encouraged to do the same.

So Rule Five comes with a proviso for spouses: Encourage us to be more involved, but don't expect that we're going to be able to easily shake off a lifetime's worth of training in domestic detachment. For many of us, the spirit is willing, but the flesh wants *Monday Night Football*. Be insistent, but gentle.

These rules are probably the best we dads can do for now. Lamentably, many companies still seem to believe that a man's family is actually in competition with his job. The truth is, of course, that fatherhood has given many of us a greater appreciation for solid workplace values such as stability and reliability and honest effort. Our children have made us grown-ups in the best sense of the word: men who are truly responsible, men who have found a purpose for working that's more important than their egos or their material gratification.

Nonetheless, in most American corporations, when you say to the senior manager, "I love my family," it tends to be decoded as "I won't do nights or weekends." Not exactly words that warm the executive heart. I wish I knew how to change the perception that the guys who sacrifice their lives to the workplace are somehow better workers than the ones who don't. But doing that is going to require a long time and a lot of fathers speaking out.

For those of us who take balancing work and family seriously, it will always be a matter of muddling along somehow. Like the women who've plunged into the workplace over the past couple of decades, we'll just have to get good at cobbling together satisfying lives for ourselves and our families, drawing from a supply of time and money that never seems like quite enough—but somehow always is.

I continue to think that the battle to make the workplace work for dads is one very much worth waging. I'd love it if an as-yet-unborn son would someday say to me, "All I can think of is how you and all the guys in your generation got cheated by not getting paternity leave for the first two months of your children's lives."

Well, I'd say, that was the way things happened back then. It's hard to understand why now, but it seemed to make sense at the time.

THE AGE OF GIVING BACK

My favorite part of the day is about eight in the evening, when Amanda and I spend our quiet time. We rock back in the big wicker chair in her bedroom. As the Barney night-light casts its faint plummy glow, we gaze at each other and she takes her bedtime bottle.

As much as I've always relished those moments with her—the faint coconut smell of her baby lotion, her rhythmic sucking at the bottle, the low creaking of the chair, the pressure of her tired head against my arm—I used to think that she got the slightly better deal. After all, she was being fed and held and loved to distraction. I was being poked in the nose.

Then, one night when she was a little more than a year old, the equation suddenly changed. She had almost finished the bottle, a fact she signaled by flinging it casually into my lap. Because I was wearing a sweater that shed, I ran my mouth over the nipple to clean it off, then put it near her lips to see whether she might not want a few gulps more. She must have thought I was hungry, because she took the bottle with both hands and held it up to my mouth, inviting me to have some.

As mawkish and overstated as this might sound, it really was one of the most remarkable moments of my life. For the first time, after nearly thirteen months of unremitting one-way devotion, Amanda had consciously decided to offer something concrete in return.

It was, in fact, just the beginning. She is now in what I think of as a golden age, the Age of Giving Back. Nowadays, scarcely a meal passes without Amanda attempting to feed Sharon or me several of her goldfish crackers or some tiny bits of apple. As we eat, she studies our faces intently. Sharon thinks she's trying to figure out how chewing works, but I have a different theory.

I've noticed the way Amanda waits until I've smiled and said, "Yum, delicious," before smiling herself. I think she's beginning to understand how gratifying it is to nurture others. While her own needs and desires still top her agenda— she would be a very strange toddler otherwise—we can see clear signs of her pronounced interest in caring for us in ways that reflect our care of her.

She reads to us, though it might not seem like reading to anyone who wasn't a parent. She sits with Sharon or me, her cousins' dog-eared copy of *The Poky Little Puppy* on her lap, and points randomly, but with great deliberateness, to words on the page. Then she recites the few letters—A, B, D, Y—that she knows, in no particular order. As she does, she looks at us to make sure we're getting the drift of her story.

Then there are the presents she gives us: a piece of onion skin that has fallen from the kitchen counter onto the floor, a tuft of lint. She places the item into the middle of our outstretched palms with infinite care, as if it's a precious offering. She looks up for thanks, gets them, and runs off screeching with happiness.

Last weekend, she fell asleep in the car as we were driving home late from her grandmother's house. When we arrived, I lifted her from the car seat while Sharon opened the door; the plan was to slip into the house and get her into bed without waking her. I placed her in the crib, then pulled down the bar so that I could lean over and kiss her good night. As I did, her eyes popped open.

She stared at me for a moment, trying to place this guy who, while extremely familiar, had not been part of her dream. Then she realized who I was. Instantly her hand reached out. She stroked my cheek lightly and comfortingly, and patted my hair, all the while looking up at me with the gravest expression on her face.

Not long after I left her bedroom, Sharon and I turned in ourselves. But while tumbling toward sleep, I found myself cast back to a moment so early in my life I didn't imagine it was possible for a person to recall it.

I'm not sure exactly how old I was, but I was in my grandparents' bedroom in Pennsylvania, and my mother had just put me down for a nap. I could smell the unlikely perfume of an elderly couple's house: roast beef and mothballs and liniment. I could see the gray light of the shuttered room, feel the wide, cottony wales of the bedspread against my cheek, hear the groan of the narrow steps—a sound so far away it was barely at the edge of hearing—as my mother went back downstairs.

Even though I was now a grown-up in a grown-up's bed, that night I slept the slow, dark, delicious sleep of a very young child.

PRESUMED INCOMPETENT: THE MYTH OF MR. MOM

It's time for a shameful confession: I've been a guest on a syndicated talk show. It was, however, just a little one, and it wasn't my fault. One of the show's producers apparently needed, on very short notice, someone with fatherhood credentials and somehow heard about some guy who worked at *Parents*. I was sweet-talked. I was told it "wasn't like the other shows."

As hard as I tried to conceal my appearance after the fact, a few friends found out. After the requisite teasing, they asked how it had gone, with the assumption that it had been either a total goof or else some sort of hideous freak show. Neither description is completely accurate, though the experience had, to be sure, elements of both. Mostly, however, I am grateful that my moment in the TV eye, for as much as I heard about it afterward, went largely and mercifully unnoticed by the American viewing public.

In retrospect, what was most unsettling about the show was the question I'd been asked to "debate" with the other guests: Can men nurture children as well as women? It is, I suspect, virtually impossible for any man who has given his heart over to his child—as if most of us have any other choice—to understand anyone even imagining such a question. And yet, there I was, having to sit in front of a camera and pretend to take it seriously.

Still, I wasn't as surprised as I probably should have been when a college kid in the studio audience whom I met after the show told me about the woman sitting next to him—matronly, neat, respectably dressed. Throughout the taping, in response to nothing in particular, she kept muttering, "Only mothers know what their children are thinking. Only mothers know what their children are thinking," as if it were some sort of mantra.

She's an extremist, certainly, but she's hardly alone in her convictions. So maybe it's time to settle this nurturing business right here and now. I am certain there's a qualitative difference between a man's emotional attitude toward his children and a woman's toward hers. I also concede that I have absolutely no idea how it feels to carry a child to term. And growing up in a typical American family, where girls played with babies while boys treated games of house as if they were conduits of deadly viruses, I understand that men haven't been taught to think of themselves as nurturers in the way that women have.

It is, nonetheless, a major stretch from those acknowledgments to the belief that women are "naturally" more nurturing than men, or that they are "better" parents, especially in the absence of a shred of empirical support for such claims. In fact, a considerable amount of research indicates clearly that men respond to an infant's needs exactly as well as women do. And children themselves respond not to a parent's gender, but to a parent's love.

However, mere logic and an overwhelming body of evidence don't seem quite enough to loosen the grip of those men and women who cling desperately to the notion of motherhood's mystique. And to its flip side: that men, for purely biological reasons, cannot be as serious, as sensitive, or as intuitively knowing about their children as women are.

Let me stress that I don't believe mothers and fathers are, or should be, interchangeable. Whether the reasons for this are cultural, biological, or passed on by spores, the truth remains that men and women are temperamentally distinct entities. We are yin and yang, or maybe peanut butter and jelly —whatever metaphor you want to plug in here, the point is that we complement each other. What I find wrongheaded is the idea that these differences make men innately inferior as parents. This notion cheats the guys who believe it out of the pleasures of family. And it cheats their kids, who don't get the fatherly attention they deserve.

This message, which I think of as the Myth of Mr. Mom, seems to be a constant, subliminal presence around us. In the movies, especially, some really peculiar ideas about fatherhood get bandied about. In *Mr. Mom*—the film that named the syndrome—the laughs come from a vision of the average American father as a man so spectacularly incompetent at the domestic arts that he leaves his kids unattended in supermarkets and makes them grilled cheese sandwiches with a steam iron; his wife, of course, can run a household effortlessly, even with three children clinging to her legs. Lest you think that I'm accusing the fair sex of unfairness, allow me to point out that *Mr. Mom* was largely put together by men.

Or take the more recent movie *Mrs. Doubtfire*—the extraordinary box office performance of which clearly has something to do with our society's hunger for good fathers. In a story that's meant to present the notion that a man can be a tender, empathetic, thoroughly competent parent, there's another implicit message: that the only way a dad can have these parental virtues appreciated is by dressing up as a woman.

Even David Williams, the Houston Oilers lineman who briefly became a media cynosure when he missed a game to be in the delivery room for his son's birth, needed to be gently put in his place. His wife kidded him on national TV for putting their newborn's diaper on backwards.

And where is this place where caring, involved fathers need to be put? Close, but not too close.

I am reminded of this almost every time Amanda and I go to the supermarket together. Even though our little safaris are loads of fun, they're not all NutraSweetness and Crystal Light. From time to time we'll get a certain look from certain women—that check-out-that-cute-baby-with-Mr.-Thinks-He's-

Alan-Alda look. Once, on the express line, I was quizzed by an older woman whose manner quickly went from graciously patronizing to brusque when it turned out that I knew not only my daughter's exact height and weight but exactly which shots she had received. (Yes, the woman actually asked, though *challenged* is probably the more accurate word.)

And then there was the memorable Saturday excursion during which Amanda became upset when I put the kibosh on a scheme of hers that involved cluster-bombing jars of Gerber from the grocery shelves onto the linoleum. I moved our grocery cart out of swatting range, and she voiced her disagreement in an extended series of enraged wails.

In an eyeblink, a middle-aged woman appeared beside our cart; I'm not sure whether she just happened to be near us or had dashed over to Amanda's aid. "Your baby's hungry," she announced.

I took the advice in a spirit of neighborliness. "Actually, I think she's just interested in the jars. I fed her less than an hour ago."

"She must not have gotten enough to eat."

"It was pretty much her usual lunch," I said, starting to feel twinges of irritation, but still inclined to give the benefit of the doubt.

"You fed her?" she asked.

"Yes."

The woman paused. "I still say she's hungry," she said, spun on her heel, and wheeled her cart away. There you have it, I thought: I'm supposed to know less about my daughter's eating habits than a woman who's never laid eyes on her before.

I've learned to hold my tongue when incidents of this sort take place, or even when well-meaning people make the assumption that as a man I am, in some basic way, ignorant about taking care of a child. Confronting others has never, in my experience, switched on any lightbulbs in their brains. Still, while in no way wishing to belittle the contribution most mothers make to their children's welfare, I feel compelled to point out that there is no magic in knowing when your child has had enough to eat, or needs to be put down for a nap, or requires comforting. It's a simple issue of competence and attentiveness. Any adult (and most children) with a little training and moderate degrees of empathy and good sense can read the signs.

This kind of good judgment is, more than anything else, an outgrowth of experience. However, in the past, our society has had a way of subtly dissuading men from gaining the hands-on experience in parenthood that's necessary to develop good judgment, thereby—voilà!—perpetuating the myth of male incompetence.

However, as many guys have figured out nowadays, the most important prerequisite for bringing children up well is not which gender you are, but what kind of parent you want to be. Now all that remains for those of us who believe this is to convince the remainder of our society to at least leave us alone and get on with our business.

I am deeply grateful that Sharon has let me be just as much a part of Amanda's life as I want to be. After a few postnatal gibes, she has almost never chided me about my missteps, even though she has been obviously tested at certain moments, like the time I tried to get Amanda into a particularly complex pair of overalls. (To be honest, she did look like a junior member of the Sex Pistols by the time I was done.) In fact, Sharon is very gracious about acknowledging, even to strangers, that Amanda is a more compliant eater for her father than for her mother.

And if my wife wants an occasional toddler-free afternoon, she simply leaves the two of us together. No moment of indecision just before she departs, as if putting her child in my care is a de facto act of negligence. No novel-length set of instructions. No hourly checkup calls. She doesn't treat me like a babysitter. She trusts me. And I appreciate it.

In fact, if Sharon had to trade places during the daytime for a week, or a month, my daughter and I would cope just fine. Amanda would be adequately fed and rested and bathed and loved. There would be no comical exploding washing machines or charred pancakes. I would not keep her up late each night watching basketball games (though I see no harm in occasionally letting her witness Patrick Ewing in action).

In a perfect world, Sharon and I would each work half-weeks and trade off Amanda's care. That way we'd each get to stay in touch with the satisfactions of working life while still getting lots of one-on-one time with our favorite daughter. Moreover, in my utopia, this arrangement would neither brand us as weirdos in the eyes of our peers nor inspire patronizing comments. Instead, it would be regarded as the norm.

And the most important thing: In this perfect world everyone, whether man or woman, would simply assume that when it comes to taking care of his child, every dad would be trusted to know what he's doing.

Is such a notion of collective good faith nothing more than an outlandish pipe dream? It might seem so in a time where bitter feelings between men and women seem epidemic. But I think there's cause for optimism on this score. The very fact that some degree of debate—albeit of a rather primitive variety—has been initiated on the subject of a man's fitness to nurture children means that it is being recognized as a possibility. That alone represents progress.

After the talk show had "wrapped"—as we like to say in the television business—I listened to snatches of the conversations from members of the studio audience. A few of them even approached us to shake hands or share a quick opinion. I came away with the overwhelming feeling that the women in the audience were more than ready to embrace the idea of involved fatherhood, even if they might not have been fully prepared to believe it.

You can't fault them for their skepticism, I guess. Involved fatherhood is barely an idea whose time has come, and already it's being turned into a cartoon. We hear so much rubbish about the New Father; he's on the cover of *Time,* he took a 50 percent pay cut so that he could be with his kids more, he's elbowing his wife out of the way so that he can feed the baby, he eats tofu and granola, he runs around in the woods nude banging on a drum, blah blah blah.

In a weird way, I envy guys who exhibit the courage it takes to court that sort of ridicule. However, ask most men with children whether they consider themselves New Fathers and you'll get little but scorn. And rightly so. Our scorn, though, is for the cliché, the label, not the reality. Ask us whether we make a point of spending more time with our children than our own fathers did, and we'll answer you overwhelmingly in the affirmative. Ask us whether we're willing to share the burdens of child care with our wives, or whether being a father has brought us a greater sense of fulfillment; you'll get a more or less identical response.

Okay, we're fathers, and we're new. But few of us care to be placed in any category that identifies us in capital letters. It implies that we've become part of a sociological trend when most of us feel that, in fact, we've made the ultimate individual choice.

That's why I don't want anyone to call me Mr. Mom, or think that my giving my daughter a bath is "cute." Nor do I appreciate any implication that wanting to tend to her is "feminine." Quite the contrary—nothing has ever made me feel more masculine, or prouder to be a man, than caring for my child.

And furthermore, when my daughter wakes in the middle of the night, terrified by something she has dreamt, she calls for her daddy. Sharon, in fact, is summarily dismissed if she enters Amanda's lair prepared to offer comfort. Amanda has decided the job belongs to me.

Is this because I'm the one she's accustomed to seeing at 3 A.M., or because it's my biological destiny?

I'll let you answer that one.

WHAT ARE LITTLE GIRLS MADE OF?

As contemporary fathers-to-be, we're pretty much expected to profess indifference to the sex of the child en route. When asked, we utter the classic line "Oh, I don't care if it's a girl or a boy, just as long as it's healthy." This is our way of demonstrating that we've shed the skin of sexism.

Well, I'm not embarrassed to say that when Sharon and I found out that we were expecting, I hoped for a boy. Okay, maybe I'm a little embarrassed. But it's still true.

I'm not sure why it mattered to me. I didn't especially care about having a male heir to ensure the world a steady supply of McCoys well into the twenty-first century. Let's face it, my ancestors are perfectly respectable and modestly accomplished people, but we're not exactly the Vanderbilts. Historians would scarcely weep at our passing. And besides, I have several male cousins who could keep the family name going if it really became a problem.

So why did I care about having a son? Part of it, I think, was looking forward to presenting a male offspring with my accumulated store of guy knowledge. I'm quite aware that there's nothing to keep a girl from grasping the principles behind chopping firewood, changing spark plugs, or executing a swinging bunt. And let the record clearly show that Sharon and I have both long been opposed to the kind of cultural segregation that pushes girls toward Barbies, boys toward G.I. Joes. Nonetheless, at the same time, the idea of passing along to your son some of the minor skills your father passed along to you does have an undeniable sentimental attraction.

Also, I was under the impression that a boy would make for a superior play partner. Ever since I've been a teenager, my idea of fun with a small child has boiled down to one word: roughhousing. Preferably followed by more roughhousing. It was probably unfortunate that I ran into my friend Carl on the street not long after finding out that my fatherhood was imminent; his son Zack was about a year and a half old at the time, and Carl was telling me how much he enjoyed coming home from work each evening and being immediately ambushed by a pint-sized professional wrestler.

"Sometimes," said Carl, "I don't even have time to get my coat off before he's grabbing my leg. In about a minute we're rolling around the floor together, I'm tickling him, he's absolutely shrieking with joy, and I totally forget my day at work."

"It sounds like heaven," I said.

"Pretty close," Carl conceded.

"But couldn't you do it just as easily with a girl?" I asked a little anxiously. This was before Sharon had had the amniocentesis done, so I was trying to cover all my bets.

Carl considered the question for a moment. "Wouldn't be the same," he then said, with a little more finality than I would have liked.

However, the primary reason I wanted our child to be male was for the conversation. Maybe this will sound a little odd, but for years before I even thought about becoming a father, there'd be certain times—during long car drives, or walking down the lane behind our house on a fall afternoon—when I found myself imagining dialogues with a child. My child.

My child would pose the questions that human beings find so crucial at a certain age (and, if they're lucky, for their entire lives). Why the seasons change. Why animals have tails but people don't. Why Aunt Eleanor's potato salad doesn't taste like Mommy's. How people can say and do such terrible things to each other. How your parents can love you while they're simultaneously punishing you. Why it gets dark at night. Why we all have to die. I would then do my best to explain these things so that my child would be—well, if not always wiser, then at least better able to bear life philosophically.

In these dialogues, my child was always a boy.

I'm not suggesting for a moment that such concerns are the sole property of my gender. I guess I just assumed my perspective would mean far less to a child whose experience would be, in many ways, incomprehensible. There were so many things I could never know about a girl's life—all of puberty, for example. I tried to comfort myself with the observation that, no matter what the gender, by the time my child was thirteen I'd be denied most routes of access into his (or her) heart. But at least with a boy I'd be able to guess what I wasn't being told.

Finally, Sharon's tests came back, and we found out that we would be parents of a girl. To my mild surprise, I wasn't crushed. The conventional wisdom turned out to be true: at the moment when it really matters, most parents honestly don't care about anything except their child being healthy and whole. And Amanda Katherine McCoy (for that was what we'd agreed to name a girl) was, from all indications, an exceedingly robust specimen.

So I spent about five minutes lamenting the father-son relationship that might have been, then decided—sagely, I think, considering that I had no choice in the matter—that the best course of action would be to simply wait and see what kind of a she she turned out to be.

Guy helped. We had a heartening conversation soon after I got the news. He'd gone through the same thing—anticipating a boy, getting a girl—just a couple of years before. "Now that it's happened," he said, "I wouldn't have it any other way. Girls are the best. I'll only warn you about one thing: A little girl is totally in control of you. She knows that you will do anything she says. So just be prepared to have the saddle on your back and the spurs digging into your side. *All the time.* Oddly enough, you'll love it."

As I said, heartening words. But not necessarily convincing. It was hard to tell whether Guy was genuinely a convert, or whether his speech was the equivalent of Napoleon allowing that, once you spent some time there, Elba actually wasn't such a bad little place.

So now, nearly two years into our life with Amanda, am I a believer? Do I wish our child had been a boy? Not if it means our child would have been anyone other than Amanda. Do I still think there's a difference between little boys and little girls? Not having much experience with little boys, it's hard to say. But I think so.

She certainly exhibits traits that we traditionally associate with femininity. Cuddling is a firm priority. On the other hand, being pinned to the living room carpet or held upside down (after a brief infatuation as an infant) are activities she seems to enjoy about as much as getting her nose suctioned with one of those bulb gizmos. As far as actual roughhousing goes, an all-fours chase around the couch that concludes in a bear hug is as rowdy as she cares to get.

Strangely, the lack of opportunity for picking on someone who is not my own size isn't in the least a disappointment. In the evenings, I have found that after a nasty and brutish— but rarely short—commute, a clinch works just as well as a half nelson to clear away the day's detritus.

Nor is Amanda inclined, for the most part, to equate anger with physical aggression, as the parents of boys so often see. On several occasions, in a fit of pique, she has been known to flail her arms at Sharon or me—she looks like the world's worst boxer—and once she even miraculously clipped her mother directly on the ear with a thrown block. But her cus-

tomary response to frustration is to give the person thwart-
ing her a tart preverbal dressing-down, following which the
offense is promptly forgotten.

Once as I was watching her play with her best friend and
next-door neighbor Max, who is seven weeks older than she,
he snatched a dinosaur doll she'd been holding. It wasn't
one of her favorite playthings, granted, but there was something remarkable in the way she responded to his clear
provocation. She squawked, then gave him a withering look,
one that unmistakably said, "If it's so important to your
ridiculous male ego to have this, then be my guest." She then
insouciantly picked up his miniature plastic basketball.

However, when Max goes after one of the blue-chip toys
(the floppy plush bear, maybe, or the doll carriage), her strategy, I've noticed, changes. She doesn't hit or scream or cry;
she just digs in and holds on to it for dear life. Her clear in-
tention is to outlast him. I'm not certain which sex is supposed to be responsible for this trait, but I'm very glad to see
it.

Other aspects of Amanda's character clearly fall into a category many would regard as masculine. There is nothing
even remotely dainty in the way she eats, though her enthusiasm for the task is a joy to behold. And despite her overall
pacifism, she will quickly and utterly, with a single mighty
swat, pulverize any tower of blocks I am foolish enough to
erect, doing so with a relish that recalls Godzilla at his very
orneriest.

And then there is her obsession with all things vehicular.
If it has wheels, whether it's our station wagon or her um-

brella stroller, to her it is a "bus," and it is a powerfully magical thing. When the three of us are in the car together, Sharon and I periodically hear a small voice coming from the back seat. "Bus," the voice says, exploding the *b,* caressing the *s.* "Bus, bus," Amanda continues, as if only this word could sum up the wondrous cosmic experience.

Sharon and I have made every attempt—short of turning ourselves into tedious ideologues—to bring Amanda up in a world that makes no assumptions about girls' interests and capacities. Of course, you never know what hidden messages you're sending. (Would we praise a boy so readily for being gentle? I *think* so.)

At a certain point you just have to tell yourself that you're making the best job you can of it. So I assume that we've given our daughter a reasonably liberated upbringing so far. As a result, to the greatest degree possible, Amanda is who she is, not what anyone wants her to be. And she is far more interesting that way.

This, finally, is the thing that probably embarrasses me most about having wanted a boy. Not that some unconscious gender prejudice was revealed, or that I picked the wrong sex. It's that in my fantasies about being the father to a boy, I wanted so much less than what I received. I underestimated the size of the gift.

I have found a delicate and peculiar thrill to being the father of a girl. For one thing, you realize that you are her first boyfriend (no tittering, please), the prism through which she'll see all men reflected for the rest of her life. She flirts with you—shamelessly, because of course she's too young to know about shame. And, in response, you kiss her and run your hands through her hair and laugh and tell her how wonderful she is and hold her tightly so that no one can ever take her away from you. I suppose Guy was right. In the most innocent way possible, I am Amanda's love slave. And glad of it.

Does she know I'm a fool for her? Of course. She plays me like a deck of cards she's marked. That doesn't matter, either.

I was mistaken in so many ways about so many aspects of being father to a girl that I may as well own up to one more. I no longer feel I've got more to say to a boy than I do to a girl. Amanda is obviously too young at this point to have developed a curiosity about the matters my phantom son and I used to discuss. However, I don't see her sex as any reason not to talk seriously with her, if and when she chooses.

In fact, I use much of the time we spend together now—she seems to be most receptive when we're taking walks—to tell her the story of how her mother and I met, and about our decidedly unconventional early dates (although I've been deliberately vague about what's actually on-screen during a John Waters movie). I've told her how much trouble she gave her mother in the delivery room, how quiet and observant she was when she came into the world. We were together for the biggest and most dazzling mystery of all, so that when she gets a little older I don't anticipate the slightest hesitation about tackling the relatively minor ones.

I'll even talk to her about guys. In fact, I sort of want to talk to her about guys. I want her to know about us—how wonderful it can be to share a life with the best of us, how the remainder can best be avoided, how to tell the two apart, why we think the way we do, which of the stereotypes about us are entirely malicious and which have a grain of truth. Men who have daughters won't think me disloyal for this; there's nothing like fathering a girl to make you realize that the allegiance to blood is greater than the one to sex. I figure that if she knows what she's getting into beforehand, she might save herself a few bad choices. That will only leave several dozen.

But there's another gift that, as a father, I can uniquely offer my daughter: I have no agenda for her, no script for her happiness. When it comes to how the life of a son should turn out, my notions would have been, in all probability, all too specific. But a girl's? Not even a glimmer. Whatever she wants is fine by me.

I ran into Carl again at a mutual friend's birthday party a few months ago. He and his wife were pregnant again. I couldn't resist asking him the usual rigmarole about finding out the baby's sex when they went for her amniocentesis. "We're still talking about that," he said. "We both have kind of mixed feelings."

"Have any preference this time around?" I asked.

He squirmed a little. "Well, I guess it would be nice to have one of each. Though I have to say, I wouldn't mind a second boy."

That's odd, I was on the verge of saying. If it were us, I wouldn't mind a second girl.

CONVERSATIONS WITH MY FATHER

One of the best descriptions of fatherhood that I ever heard came from a guy who worked in the office next to mine at a former job. He said it made him feel "as if I've been handed the baton for my lap in a never-ending generational relay race."

Okay, so it's a little portentous. But I do know what he was saying. Among fatherhood's myriad benefits, one of the most pleasing is the kinship that I now feel with every man who was ever a parent. Very much including my own father, even though he died more than twenty years ago.

I'm always surprised to hear new dads say that their own fathers were useless as role models. Not that there aren't some men whose child-rearing efforts aren't worth repudiating. But denying the influence of our fathers does little, it seems to me, to keep us from treating our kids very much as we were treated, whether we're conscious of it or not. Doing what our parents do is probably our first habit—a reflex, really—and arguably the one that's hardest to break.

Sometimes that reflex tells a man that he should feel injured or angry when his child displays a contrary will. Or that it's impossible for a father to have as strong an emotional bond with his child as a mother does. Or that his child's life will be fraught with failure if he doesn't make that child sufficiently competitive and hard-nosed. Whatever your upbringing was like, your father provided the script for the role you have assumed. You can modify it. You can even deliberately set out to be the exact opposite when it comes to child-rearing. But you can't discard that script.

For present purposes, let's set aside the issue of psychodads—the drunks, the abusers, the criminal types. The challenges such a man offers to a son who in turn becomes a father are, to put it mildly, prodigious. However, this kind of father is relatively rare, and I'm not really equipped to talk about pathological characters.

I'd rather focus on the sort of father most of us had, the one who was well-meaning and imperfect—as well-meaning and imperfect as we are, in fact. A man who always intended to follow through on his good intentions, but didn't always manage it. A man who wanted nothing more than our happiness, but didn't listen to us as much as he might have. A man who tried hard not to push us so that he could live through our achievements, but couldn't entirely resist the temptation. A man we loved and sometimes feared, but didn't fully respect.

As those of us who knew that kind of father can tell you,

understanding his legacy involves *work*. You've really got to sift through the past with a scholar's eye, examining everything he did, right and wrong, so that you can use the good stuff and sidestep the bad. It's like conducting an archaeological dig; you comb through layers of your memory looking for often fragile or partial clues to a former civilization. You're not sure what you'll turn up, but you know that if your approach to the work is lazy, there's a good chance you'll miss a crucial piece of the puzzle.

Doing all this spadework is, to be sure, laborious, but it gives you at least one great advantage as a new father—the more you understand how your dad went about the job, the better position you're in to improve upon it. You illuminate your own parental choices by giving yourself a history, a context. You tend not to merely react.

This, anyway, is the conclusion I came to in the months after Amanda's birth, after spending a long time thinking about my own very decent but deeply flawed father.

Although I've spent more than half my life without him, I haven't ever stopped loving him. Over a period of years, granted, I gradually found myself thinking about him less often than I used to. However, when Amanda was born, he became a strong and constant presence in my life again. It took becoming a father myself to finally come to terms with what he meant to me—which is not the same thing as wanting to be exactly the father he was.

What has really helped our relationship is that we're talking again.

I don't mean this in any supernatural sense. He doesn't

appear before my eyes in an undulating veil of smoke and speak in an echo-laden voice. He's no special effect. When I feel the need for his conversation, I can summon him more or less deliberately; after all these years, the sound of his voice is still imprinted on my memory, and so is his Socratic turn of mind. I appreciate both of them more than I used to.

During his lifetime, there were two particular sources of resentment toward my dad that I could never shake. They're mundane things, I readily admit. But because they were un-resolved at the time of his death, when I was fifteen, they have continued to occupy the part of me that has never got-ten over being fifteen.

One complaint is, in retrospect, just silly. It was the way he always sent me straight to the barbershop the moment my hair began to tickle the tops of my ears. I probably don't need to remind any man who grew up in the sixties or sev-enties what a loaded issue hair length was between fathers and sons, and how much more it had to do with perceived moral decay than follicular hyperactivity.

The other cause of strife between us was a little more se-rious. It had to do with his insistence on pushing me toward a definition of worldly success that I didn't believe in. The real pressure started when our family went to Europe for three weeks—I was eleven then—and I foolishly assigned myself the task of translating foreign prices into dollars. To me it was simply a responsibility I could competently meet, as well as a chance to indulge an eleven-year-old's typical fascination with money. To my father, it became the inspira-tion for a dream that, in turn, became the curse of my preadolescent life: that one day his son would become an international banker.

His death came four years after that trip, almost three years after his cancer was diagnosed. In that time scarcely a month passed without my hearing the words *international banker.* (Somewhere along the line, the dream sprouted a subplot: I would be accepted into the U.S. Naval Academy. He was, it goes without saying, a Navy man.)

From dairy farmer to small business man (Dad owned a men's store) to financier in three generations—now, *that* was his idea of a family history. Not mine, though. I was almost ridiculously ill suited to the destiny he had fitted out for me. The world back then seemed squarely (if you'll forgive the word) in the middle of a social eruption that would surely result in the takeover of the world by the young and hairy. Meanwhile, I was developing into a pretty good lead guitarist in the Keith Richards mold. I didn't want a degree in economics and a pin-striped suit. I wanted a powerful amp and a world without bankers.

Unappetizing scenes would no doubt have taken place had my father and I ever gotten the chance to debate our differences. But we didn't. By the time I knew what I wanted, he had started dying, and it didn't seem right to make him feel worse about things than he already did. So I went along, and sort of hated myself for going along, and sort of hated him for forcing me to sort of hate myself. And that's the way it stayed until the very end.

I won't dwell on his physical suffering or the details of his death; I'll say only that his final years held more pain than anyone should be put through. To the best of my knowledge, I felt no responsibility for his illness, as children sometimes irrationally do. No, the nature of my self-recrimination was quite different—that at a time when he badly needed closeness, I was doing what every teenager instinctively does with his parents: I was making tracks in the other direction. The week he died, I remember, I spent most of the time playing the second Led Zeppelin album, which had just come out. Lying on the bedroom floor with the portable speakers smack against my ears, I could hear everything. My mother wasn't about to object to my taste in music, not at that moment. I finally felt free. I also felt as if my insides had been hollowed out.

By the time Amanda was born, some two decades on, I'd had a few major life experiences in common with my dad. Marriage, obviously. But in addition, we'd both started businesses; his had been succeeding until he got sick, while my plans had failed to pan out. Nonetheless, we both knew what it was like to take a major risk for the sake of our families. And, most crucially, we both knew how it felt to hold *our* babies in our arms.

One night, when Amanda was a few months old, I placed her limp form in the crib and was sitting in the darkened nursery breathing in its talcumed perfume, rocking in the chair where I'd just lulled her to sleep, when my father's voice came softly. I guess I'd been thinking about him without realizing it, and my thoughts became his words.

He was asking me if I would forgive him.

Of course I would, I finally said. Upon giving the question

serious thought, it no longer made any sense to blame him because he wanted me to win at life, although I told him I still didn't completely buy into his notion of what constituted winning. Also, over the years I had discovered things about myself for which he deserved a lot of the credit. Like his making me care about doing things well, something for which I will never stop being grateful because it has helped me gain a degree of success—according to *my* definition.

In addition, I expressed to my father a degree of gratitude for the negative example he'd provided. (This, of course, would have been too harsh to say if we'd *really* been talking.) As she grows up, I told him, Amanda will be encouraged to make her own decisions according to what gives *her* a sense of fulfillment—not that in her brief time on earth so far, she has shown the slightest inclination to let others make her decisions for her. But when it came to letting him off the hook, I gladly agreed. It was clear that hoarding trivial resentments from adolescence was purposeless. It was something a child might do, but not . . . well, not a *father.*

It was interesting that the question of whether he'd forgiven me never came up. I simply assumed he had.

Maybe a couple of weeks after the first encounter, I was straightening up around my office one evening when I started thinking about how when I was a child, I used to wish my father could be different. Not richer or more athletic or more famous, but *happier.* I would wish that when our family hit a rough patch, he'd stop shouldering more of the blame than was strictly necessary. That he wouldn't allow himself to feel pushed and pushed—by us, by my mother, by his work—until finally he would flame out and administer a senseless spanking over some misdemeanor my sister or I had committed. That he wouldn't get so blue when he drank. That he wouldn't drink.

In fairness, he wasn't the kind of guy who got liquored up nightly and then fell apart. His relationship with alcohol was occasional. He was just one of those people who should've never gotten near the stuff. As Sharon once observed of a mutual acquaintance, "He drinks not to enjoy himself." That was my dad, sorry to say.

As I was remembering all this, his voice appeared again, and it asked a politely phrased, unduckable rhetorical question: "How can you separate the things you didn't like about me from the things that made you think I was a good father?" Because I *did,* in the end, despite everything, think of him as a good father. That's why instead of hating him for his faults, I was sad for him.

His question made me wonder: If it *had* been possible for him to undergo some sort of personality surgery at my direction, if all his defects could have been snipped away, would the procedure also remove the virtues I so admired and tried to emulate?

Could he have lost his compulsion to take on too much responsibility, and still held on to his unshakable belief in the value of hard work? Would he have still had the courage to dream big without having any big dreams for me? Was it possible to remove his embarrassing insistence on absolute honesty and loyalty to the people around him—and naively expecting the same in return—without turning him into a conniving liar?

"You've made your point, Dad," I whispered to the room.

105

As a result of these conversations, and several more like them, I've made a deal with my father. I agree to understand that he did his misguided best, and he agrees to allow me to do my misguided best. I am trying not to take the world's weight on my shoulders as he did, although this is hard to avoid when you grow up thinking that's what men do—in the same way I have grown up thinking I have no choice but to be hard-working and honest, and that hard-working, honest guys ultimately find themselves ill-used and disillusioned.

But my father is helping me with these things. He keeps telling me I don't have to make his mistakes.

I'm happy that I can give him—in addition to the kind of candid, collegial, ego-free adult relationship we never had the chance to develop in real life—a granddaughter who will never know him, but will feel his presence in ways she couldn't recognize. It goes beyond the particular curve of the upper lip that he has passed on to her, or the picture of him that sits amid the family photos in her room. It also goes beyond my resolve that Amanda embrace many of the values that my dad was resolved I would embrace. His influence on my family has already taken forms so varied and subtle they're often not immediately detectable.

I realized this during a visit to my mother's house not long after Amanda was born. As Sharon and I were going through an album of family snapshots, we came upon a picture of my father, sitting in "his" chair in our living room in Baltimore and holding my sister, who couldn't have been more than a few months old—very close, in fact, to Amanda's age at that point. What struck me about this picture were his eyes. He looked so awestruck and grateful as he gazed at his sleeping child. Seeing him this way, I felt a sudden glow spread through me; generations of McCoy men were mirrored in that face. For a delicious moment, it felt as if he were still alive.

That's why it saddens me when I hear men say that their fathers are (or were) worthless. Worthless fathers obviously exist, but even the worst of them, it seems to me, can make his son a better father; the most negative example is still an example. We never start from scratch—there are too many of those invisible early lessons echoing in our brains for that to be true. But that doesn't mean we're helpless to change. It's important to remember that we can control, to a large extent, the shape of our family's life.

If you were unfortunate enough to have had a father who slapped you around, you're not predestined to do the same to your own kids. The temptation will almost certainly be there, but you've got other choices. Likewise, if your dad kept his emotional distance as you were growing up, you're not obliged to uphold the family tradition. The reason such traits are passed on from generation to generation isn't because they work. It's because they're never questioned, or because we can always find rationalizations for them.

When the time comes for each man to assume the role of father, we all really ought to have a few discussions—preferably imagined, in some cases—with our dads. There's no script so good that it can't do without a little editing. And you can only rewrite the bad ones, because it's too late to throw them out. But either way, you and your memories of your own upbringing need to become collaborators.

And you must have the final editorial say. The only other person with any influence should be your spouse. Relatives, friends, and people like me who write books are entitled to float their opinions, but the real power has to reside in you.

Having arrived at a rapprochement with my dad, I feel a whole lot better about my ability to rear a child. To shift metaphors abruptly, I no longer have the need—as I often did, especially before Amanda came into our lives—to be the perfect navigator of my family. My father, for all his wild-goose chases and minor accidents, might have put a few dents in my psychic chassis, but they don't seem to have made me undrivable.

Of course, I will try to make fewer mistakes than he did, and I may succeed. I will also sometimes foul things up in ways he couldn't even have dreamed of. That's how it goes when you come from a race of imperfect creatures.

There is only one thing that frightens me—that, like him, I won't live to see my daughter reach adulthood. In the last weeks of my father's life, as he lay in a hospital bed woozy from painkillers and shrunken and ashy from sickness, he would look at my sister and me, and he'd weep. His lower lip stuck out like a toddler's. He would say, over and over, that the hardest part of dying was leaving us behind when we were so young. He would never get to see us graduate from college, he said. He would never get to see me become an international banker.

It scares me to think about the end of my father's life. I feel in my bones that worry made him sick and eventually killed him. And I have inherited his capacity for worry. However, this is another of the problems he and I have been discussing lately. He's extremely confident that I can beat it.

INVITATION TO THE DANCE

I've already mentioned my daughter's early—possibly even prenatal—appreciation for the recorded output of Tito Puente. What I failed to add, however, is that our two A.M. whirls around the living room to the scorching timbale solo in "Ran-Kan-Kan" were just the beginning. It's hard to know exactly how this happened, but Amanda has blossomed into a card-carrying go-go girl.

Whatever the cause might be, it's certainly not genetic. One of the strongest bonds between Sharon and me is our shared distaste toward the very thought of dancing in public. Safely at home, with the shades drawn and the door locked, we might possibly have slow-danced very closely once or twice, employing certain sections of the anatomy in a style somewhat indelicately known as grinding. Then again, we might not have.

110

On the rare occasions—weddings, notably—when getting out on the floor becomes a social necessity, we mask our embarrassment by indulging in ironic versions of the Jerk or the Swim or the Hitchhiker. Or, at one sub-memorable reception, the Freddie (though Sharon, to her credit, had the sense to steer clear of *that* one). My manner of dancing to fast songs has been compared, with regrettable accuracy, to the Funky Chicken as performed by a real chicken.

It's too early to know whether Amanda will surpass us in grace, though you'd hope she would aim a little higher than that. Right now, she expresses her love of dance not so much by actually dancing, but by the enthusiasm she brings to being a partner. Specifically, *my* partner.

Back when she was very small and lacking in bravery toward the physical world, there were certain records she wouldn't dance to. I tried her out on Chopin polonaises, but the combination of twirling and being swung up and down petrified her. Bob Marley, on the other hand, was a little too languid for her tastes; the only way you can really cut a rug to reggae with a baby in your arms is to bob straight up and down, which quickly bores a child of any discernment.

In her toddlerhood, though, she has learned to like just about any kind of music as long as you can move to it. She's crazy about this tape a friend of ours brought back from Argentina. I know as much about the art of the tango as Janet Jackson knows about square dancing, but when I lampoon the rose-in-the-teeth moves from the movies while extending Amanda's arm and holding her closely to me, it works just fine for her. She's also fond of songs that permit her to jitterbug, although her version of the step is pretty much restricted to twirling around on the floor until she starts to stagger.

Last week we were watching *Sesame Street* when a segment came on showing a group of African-American kids with painted tribal faces dancing as a Zairean soukous band laid down a loping, propulsive beat. As soon as the drummers started up, Amanda began nodding her head in a very rough approximation of the rhythm. I picked her up, and we commenced to spend a decidedly funky several minutes.

We went through all our classic moves: The Oarsman, in which, holding her perpendicular to the floor, I push her body slightly down and away from me, then tilt her back up at the end; the Broom, which features me swinging her dangling legs from side to side as if I'm brushing off a sidewalk with them; the Peek-a-Boo, a move where I rotate her so that on alternating beats she is either looking over my shoulder or staring right into my face; the Kangaroo (you can pretty much imagine this one from the title); and all the others. Amanda's screams of pleasure brought her mother into the room; the look on Sharon's face upon catching us in the act was pretty much what you'd expect from a woman who has just discovered that her daughter shares the father's gene for mental instability.

There's only one kind of dancing Amanda hasn't really cottoned to: slow-dancing. Whenever I try it, she grunts and kicks until I lower her back to the ground. When she's out there on the dance floor, she wants action, motion, excitement. She wants to be thrilled. To be sure, she's just as desirous of affection as the next toddler—it's just that she prefers a dynamic, bouncy embrace to a mushy, static one.

In the end, I'm deeply appreciative that my daughter has already learned to make a clear distinction between dancing and romancing. Of course, my gratitude might have something to do with having recently heard my friend Alan's blow-by-blow account of his daughter's fourteenth birthday party. Just in case you're the new father of a daughter, I'll spare us both the details.

I will say, though, that after listening to Alan's harrowing tale, there's one thing I've got to admit. I sure wish that when we were that age, we'd thought of something as diabolically simple as removing the lightbulbs in the basement rec room.

IN PRAISE OF IMPERFECTION

Three doors down from us on Oakwood Drive lived the Jardines. Mrs. Jardine was perhaps best known among the kids in our neighborhood for her performance at Halloween.

It wasn't that she got dressed up in full regalia and pounced on us from the bushes when we rang her doorbell. Nor did she spiff up her foyer with phony cobwebs and colored lights and play spooky music on the stereo. It wasn't even that her selection of candy was any more extravagant than the other mothers'. (In case you were wondering about Mr. Jardine: A father's role at Halloween basically consisted of chasing away the older kids when they tried to soap your windows.)

In fact, Mrs. Jardine's engagement with our favorite pagan celebration was not what made her memorable in our eyes. It was her lack of it.

She was the wife of an academic, and while no doubt a charming and intelligent woman, she had virtually no aptitude or desire when it came to dealing with children who were not her own. She wasn't even all that crazy about having neighborhood kids in her house. In all the years that I knew her son Kenny, who was a couple of years older, I couldn't have been allowed in his room on more than two or three occasions. And that was more than most of the other kids had seen of Casa Jardine. She wasn't mean, just distant and uncomfortable.

However, Halloween was the one night of the year we couldn't be avoided. In retrospect, I imagine she must have put herself through rigorous preparation for the event. Quite possibly she read several books purporting to explain the mysteries of communicating with children. Maybe she chatted with a child psychologist. Mild sedation might also have been involved.

In any case, by the time we reached the Jardines' door in our seasonal getups, she was steeled. Before we even got a chance to shout "Trick or treat!" she opened the door. She would fix all of us with an impassive stare, saying, "Goodness me. Look at this scary pirate, and this ghost, and this devil. I'd better get them some candy before they play a trick on me."

Strategically speaking, there was nothing wrong with this little speech feigning terror; the way we figured things, it was more or less our due. The problem was the totally affectless, monotonal way she uttered her lines. She sounded like the Second Victim in a community theater production of *Dracula*. And when she proffered the wooden bowl of doughnuts (Doughnuts? For Halloween? Can there be any doubt she was out of her depth?), it looked as if she were trying to impersonate a mechanical butler. Twenty years later I caught *The Stepford Wives* on TV, sat bolt upright, and gasped: Mrs. Jardine!

I think of her, poor woman, whenever someone who has gotten wind of the fact that I work for *Parents* asks me what "method" they should use to goad a finicky eater into scarfing down those peas or to potty-teach their child. Quite apart from the fact that asking me for any kind of advice is a de facto admission of desperation, I can't help but feel that it's a mistake for parents to place more stress on techniques than on the spirit in which they're offered.

There are, to be sure, strategies that have proven quite useful for helping children reach developmental goals or solve behavioral difficulties. But I feel our generation of parents often places too much faith in methods, while retaining only trace elements of confidence in our innate abilities.

Fathers, I think, are especially prone to doubts about their fitness as parents—perhaps because so many of us, lacking involved dads of our own, are flying by the seat of our pants. But I don't think that fear of imperfection is by any means exclusively a fatherhood problem. Women, too, are haunted by the prospect of being unwittingly horrible parents, of inflicting gruesome damage on their children's psyches by yielding to tenderness when they should be stern (or vice versa), by treating delicate sensibilities roughly through ignorance, by making light of their children's serious concerns, or whatever.

It's no wonder we're so terrified. Everywhere you turn, bad parents are on prominent display. Incest survivors clog the daytime talk shows. Celebrity offspring churn out books snitching on their egomaniacal, emotionally brutish moms or dads. Newspapers continually serve up sickening tales of infants beaten to death or left in dumpsters. It's very possible these days to meet a guy at a casual gathering and, within minutes of your introduction, hear the story of his relationship with an alcoholic, abusive parent.

Of course, from time to time we are blessed with brief, delicious moments when the debris of modern society seems momentarily to have settled, and a perfumed silence descends upon the earth. Then Roseanne gives another interview.

I'm not saying that anyone's individual testimonies is false, or that it doesn't take courage to make a painful, broken life public. It's just that the aggregate result of all these awful stories is that a collective bad smell has gathered around parenthood itself. When the focus is so relentlessly on those parents who have gotten it spectacularly wrong, when dysfunction starts to be seen not as an aberration but as the norm, we can easily start to think that we're somehow responsible not merely for bringing up our children, but also in some way for redeeming the institution of parenthood—even as we're hearing how inadequate we are to the task.

I remember that in the days right before Amanda was born, the notion of holding her in my male meat hooks alarmed me. What if I botched it? What if I unknowingly supported her neck in a way that practically guaranteed future spinal injury? And perhaps worst of all, what if she sensed I didn't really know what I was doing? Even after her birth, the first few times I took her in my arms were uneasy moments.

Then, one night maybe four or five days after we brought her home, we'd just finished having a single celebratory beer with our neighbors, when I suddenly heard Amanda's squalls coming from the bassinet upstairs. Without thinking, I went to her, picked her up, and cradled her. Click. Her chin nestled into my shoulder, her head fit perfectly in the crook of my neck, her unimaginably small body molded itself to my chest. A piece sliding into a puzzle.

And all it took to succeed was to put my self-doubt on hold for a moment and let my instincts do the work.

Given the current prevailing air of paranoia, a risk-free, by-the-book parenthood sounds like a pretty sensible choice. But it comes at a cost, for both parents and children. I once heard a noted child psychologist claim that one of the biggest differences he noticed between our generation and the previous one is that our moms and dads—and theirs, too, for that matter—believed their instincts alone were enough to make them good parents. Dr. Spock's famous book became a perennial bestseller, he maintained, not because it told parents how to compensate for their inadequacies, but because it helped them improve upon the basically good job they were already doing.

No doubt many escapees from lousy families would take issue with their parents' self-assessment. But, the psychologist went on to say, what we've got nowadays, instead of the blithe confidence that we innately know what's best for our

118

kids, is an absence of faith in ourselves that is, finally, just as unexamined. We're far more likely to put our trust in experts than in ourselves.

There is actually a kernel of sense in our generation's quest for information. Nobody seriously believes (I hope) that knowing more about what makes kids tick makes you a *worse* parent. It quite probably makes you a lot better. What concerns me is the assumption that we're not good enough to begin with.

I think children deal with our ignorance much more readily than they do with our fear of failure. Give this a moment's thought: If you were an infant, would you be more comforted by a parent who responded to your wails immediately and clung to you in an evident state of panic as he tried to calm you down, or a parent who maybe arrived cribside a few moments later but smiled and spoke in a low, reassuring voice that made you feel that shrieking at the top of your lungs was perhaps something of an overreaction?

This isn't meant as a defense of actual negligence. I'm just floating the notion that there may be more accurate gauges of our devotion to our children than slavish, anxiety-fueled obedience.

I am absolutely convinced that we don't need to handle every situation as if we've memorized the manual. Children are remarkably resilient. But they really don't need some parent who's going to hold them to the same neurotic ideal of perfection that the parent has swallowed wholesale.

It's hard to find the fun in your child (or anything else, for that matter) if you're fixated on doing everything correctly. And I can't think of a single emotional gift that any of us can give a child that's more crucial than the sense that their presence pleases us endlessly.

Granted, it's hard to see the joy in parenthood at certain moments—when, for example, your child has been refused the use of your toothbrush while you're in the middle of your morning toilette, and she sees fit to turn crimson and do a convincing version of a Civil Defense siren. However, the longer I am a parent and the more I learn about what makes toddlers behave the way they do, the easier it is to keep from getting my knickers in a twist when Amanda erupts. That, to me, is the single most significant role child development information plays in my life: It convinces me that 75 percent of the daily things that concern most parents aren't worth a second thought.

Of course I still brood. Am I being overindulgent? Should I be more sympathetic while she's having a meltdown, or should I totally ignore her? Do I need to spend more time telling her the names for things, or am I already too wrapped up in force-feeding her knowledge? This sort of fretting is par for the course. But the fact that we care enough about the job to question ourselves about how well we're doing it is by itself an excellent sign. And we should never forget that our children are always delighted to give us the benefit of the doubt. Love may not be enough, but I firmly believe that it's almost always close to enough.

Sure, it's a good thing to know a few techniques for getting through to children. It also makes sense to have a rudimentary knowledge of their developmental stages, as well as their mental and emotional sophistication, social maturity, and probable attention span. As my friend, the child psychologist, says, "Probably the best parent is the one who trusts most of his instincts and pays enough attention to his kids that he knows which instincts he's right not to trust."

I'm utterly certain that I have made numerous mistakes as a father. The precise nature of these mistakes probably won't be clear to me for several years at least, maybe not until Amanda is grown. However, she's a smart little girl. Whatever they are, she'll survive them.

As my friend Rich puts it, "If you're going to be a good father, you've got to know the music *and* the lyrics." Well, yes, but none of us nails all the notes every time, and it is a rare parent who doesn't from time to time flub a line. The unfortunate Mrs. Jardine had the words down cold, but the music of children eluded her. If only she'd been able, just for a moment, to still the voices of doubt inside her, she would have heard us as clear as bells.

IN DEFENSE OF OZZIE NELSON

A few months ago I was working with some of my fellow *Parents* editors on a fatherhood poll that was scheduled to appear in an upcoming issue. We were just putting the finishing touches to it when someone suggested ending the survey with something light, a parlor-game question—maybe something about which father in public life respondents most admired.

It was an unfortunate brainstorm. For the next hour, we wracked our brains in a fruitless attempt to come up with a list of choices who would fit the description. Bill Clinton? Bill Cosby? Arnold Schwarzenegger? Homer Simpson? Even the worthy candidates didn't seem like obvious choices. In semi-desperation I called several friends and said, "Name a well-known figure who comes to mind when you think of fatherhood." No one could come up with a single example.

After another editorial meeting, we all decided the smartest idea was to ask respondents who they'd cast as lead in the movie of their life, then leave a blank space. We didn't really want to resort to this; it would give profound distress to the company tabulating the results—and, purely coincidentally, run up the magazine's bill in a major way. However, we had no idea what a mess we'd created until the president of the polling firm called me a few days after receiving the eight thousand or so responses.

Everything was going just fine, he assured me with professional geniality—except for this one little thing. It was that last question. A pained sound crept into his voice. It seemed that of the first 150 or so forms that had been tallied, that question had elicited 71 different responses. The top vote getter had a grand total of four. (The final Top Ten included Kevin Costner—the winner—Tom Hanks, Mel Gibson, Dustin Hoffman, Steve Martin, Harrison Ford, and Jimmy Stewart.)

Because the answers obviously weren't going to tell us anything very definitive, he continued, might his people be permitted to strike that particular question? I told him to count the first thousand, then stop. The response, I said, was already telling me a lot.

The main thing the answers indicated was something I'd suspected for a long time—that popular culture no longer serves the cause of fatherhood as it did back in the fifties and sixties, when we had our clear pick of dads as role models. Then, it was practically impossible to switch on a television set without glimpsing a male icon who stood as an example to America's families.

And especially to America's boys, who inevitably compared their own dads to the ones on TV—just as, on some subconscious level, I'm convinced that we who are fathers today compare our own performances to those turned in by those video patriarchs of yesteryear. So it behooves us, I think, to stop for a moment here and give these guys some serious consideration.

No two TV dads, when you examine them closely, were quite alike. (Although, let's face it, they weren't all that different, either.) The favorite in our household was Jim Anderson of *Father Knows Best;* I think it was because he seemed to actually like his kids. You could tell that only with reluctance would he buckle down and administer some discipline—not that his qualms ever stopped him.

Ward Cleaver, on the other hand, always seemed to get some secret, slightly unsavory pleasure out of being an authoritarian. His little talks in the study when Beaver broke a window and then lied about it were, on the surface, stern if understanding. However, simmering just underneath was a moral smugness that even a five-year-old like me could detect. Ward didn't seem like the kind of guy who'd have ever enjoyed roughhousing with the Cleaver boys when they were younger—it would've been much too undignified.

Then there was that skinny guy on *Lassie* with the shapeless hat and the pipe—now *there* was a nonstarter. I remember him as an odd, vaguely distracted sort who would wander off by himself for several hours, return in the nick of time to rescue Timmy from the scrape of the week, then act as the mouthpiece for that episode's lesson. (It was generally either to be honest or to avoid risks, if I recall correctly.) Occasionally they'd show him interrupted by Timmy as he was baling hay or performing some other generic farm chore, but you weren't really sure how he spent his time around Rancho Lassie. I have once or twice found myself wondering what he *really* grew for a living, and whether some of whatever it was might not have found its way into his pipe.

But out of them all, the guy I personally considered the quintessence of pop culture fatherhood was Ozzie Nelson. That buffoon? None other. He provided American families with a perspective on the role that was in many ways truer than any offered by his brethren. Ozzie was, when all was said and done, the TV dad I would have wanted for my own.

I know what you're thinking: What can today's fathers possibly learn from a man whose life consisted in its entirety of hanging around the house in a cardigan, throwing himself into such life-or-death matters as whether David or Ricky should get the car on Friday night or how he could manage to sneak off for a round of golf without Harriet finding out?

Okay, so he wasn't exactly a Mensa chapter president, but he did have certain undeniable virtues. Easy Ozzie was supremely mellow at those times when he wasn't entangled in some domestic matter of mind-numbing triviality. And when he was faced with a family problem, Oz dealt with it head-on. He listened to his kids before delivering a judgment. He agonized over decisions, deploying his limited brainpower in an effort to be fair to everyone—although it was clear he took even less pleasure in issuing his verdicts than he did in deliberating over them.

Other television fathers glided through the waters of life like ocean liners, sure of themselves and their roles. Ozzie

Nelson's tugboat sputtered along, made a lot of noise, and coughed up billows of smoke. But it always arrived somewhere. And for all of us children who loved our dads despite already having made a full accounting of their imperfections, there was more of the truth of our family life—not so much the substance of it, but the dynamics—to be found among the Nelsons than in, say, those shrink-wrapped zombies from *The Donna Reed Show*.

What I found particularly laudable in Ozzie was the encouragement he offered to Ricky in his son's dream to become a rock and roll demigod. This was a remarkable feat of paternal tolerance, taking place as it did in an era when phrases such as "the devil's music" and "lewd rhythms" were tossed around without irony. (If the Nelsons were around today, Ricky would no doubt be defanging gangsta rap.) Furthermore, Ozzie supported his child's against-the-grain ambitions without even a hint of self-satisfaction. When you think about it, for somebody who was supposed to be a putz, Ozzie was a stand-up guy.

He also seemed to have, on the whole, a healthier marital relationship than did his peers. Beneath all the cute squabbling about domestic chores and spending habits necessary to any TV family of the fifties (and still, weirdly, to today's tube clans), you got the idea that Harriet actually loved Ozzie. Not that she considered him such a catch that she was blinded to his flaws, or that she stood by him because that's what wives did for their providers back then. Just that she *loved* the sweet goof.

I can't help thinking it'd be a fine thing if every household displayed the sort of unqualified acceptance of its members, foibles and all, that the Nelsons did. If you wanted to be a pint-sized Elvis, twitching lip and all, your parents would stand by you—or at least they would if they were Ozzie and Harriet. And if you bumbled and sputtered and spent large blocks of time obviously clue-free, your kids would still listen to you and respect you. What could be more assuring to a parent, or a child, than that sort of deal?

Examples of the kind of tolerance Oz and his family displayed in everyday life are in desperately short supply today. Of course, we can't go back in time to the world the Nelsons occupied. And the fictional men—as opposed to our own dads, of course—most likely to show us what it meant to be a father are dinosaurs. But no one has taken up the slack.

Today, unless you watch sitcoms, you won't find many remotely acceptable standard-bearers for contemporary fatherhood. In fact, you won't find many even if you do. The only TV character I see grappling with real issues on a regular basis and trying to do a pretty good job of it is Dan Conner on *Roseanne*. But he's more or less the oasis in a Mojave of stereotyped men—simpering studs, blue-collar boobs, and Sensitive Guys who never met a family crisis that couldn't be solved by a Great Big Hug. (Of course, there's also Bill Cosby, but he falls into a chronologically awkward place—I was too old to identify with his kids, but too young to identify with him. Besides, his moral certainty always intimidated me a little. And his show is long gone.)

And few of today's characters—the major exception is, again, Dan Conner—seems especially motivated by a love of fatherhood, the way that TV dads from another era did. Again and again, the message our popular culture seems determined to drive home is that fatherhood is an accident, a thankless (or hapless) responsibility marked by the surrender of one's free, unbounded male spirit to an emasculating world. This notion would be laughably dim-witted if it weren't so destructive, not only to our society, but to the souls of the men who buy into it.

I don't for a moment imagine we could rid the world of absentee deadbeat dads and uninvolved dads simply by putting half a dozen models of paternal rectitude on the tube. But maybe there wouldn't be quite so many failed fathers if we—both as a culture and as individuals—gave men a collective thumbs-up when they try to do a decent job bringing up their kids. (Women, too, for that matter.)

I'm not talking about a grand, showy gesture here. Most men would find that embarrassing. A genuinely felt acknowledgment might be enough to do the trick—that, and just a few more guys on television who are really like us, quietly devoted to their families and doing their best to muddle through life. Then we might have enough admirable fathers to include in a multiple-choice question.

Okay, I admit that on a certain level, it's comforting that the dearth of pop culture models gives me the freedom to be the sort of father I think is best for my daughter, without her drawing invidious comparisons between me and Jim Anderson. And it's also true that what matters more is not whose example *we* follow, but the small people who follow ours.

Still, it would be nice once in a while if we real-life role models could take a breather and let some doofus in a cardigan show us how things should *really* be handled.

GIANT STEPS

Spring has recently arrived, and Amanda and I have developed a new ritual. After Sharon goes out on her Saturday errands, my daughter and I sit down to a light lunch. Then we bop around to a couple of records just to settle the digestion. (Her two current favorites: *Muppet Beach Party* and, weirdly, Paul McCartney's *Ram.)* Then we get down to the real business of the afternoon—our walk.

I'm not talking about a promenade around the neighborhood in a stroller. Amanda will put up with being wheeled about if we're in a shopping mall or airport, but when it comes to our neighborhood, she must travel on foot. This is not negotiable.

Even as I'm slipping her arms into her denim jacket, she knows what's coming. "Walk?" she asks in a way I would consider disingenuous if she weren't seventeen months old. She stands by the door and strains for the knob, while looking expectantly over her shoulder at me.

Once we get down the hill from our driveway to the road—our street is a little too rural for sidewalks—she hits her stride, literally.

All around us spring is happening in a noisy, garish way. The smell of earth is rich and raw. Brilliant green crocus fingers sprout from the ground. Our neighbor's forsythia bushes are a lemony blur. The horses tear around the paddocks, rolling in the mud, snorting and clomping around. The birds chatter a winter's worth of southern gossip. Amanda pays none of it any heed. She wraps her hand around my index finger and grips it so tightly the nail turns crimson. She concentrates on her scuffling feet as she alternates them. She is working hard to establish a rhythm, a uniform gait, a walk that truly qualifies as a big girl's.

She still has to give it a fair bit of attention; the one-foot-in-front-of-the-other thing is getting smoother, but doesn't yet come effortlessly. "Such a good walker!" I say. "Such a fine job of walking!" She looks up, gives me a self-satisfied little smirk, and says, "Yes," in that precise, vaguely Eloise-like way of hers. Then she immediately returns her attention to the job at hand.

By the time we get back to our front steps—which she insists on taking upright with only one of my hands to steady her—we have covered the better part of half a mile. (I wouldn't have believed it, either, but I measured it by car odometer.) Far from being winded by the effort, Amanda heads straight for her mini-trike and spends another ten or fifteen minutes locomoting around the living room. She is, quite obviously, drunk on mobility.

I can't tell you how happy it makes me to see all this. It means that she is—maybe not literally, but close enough—following in her father's footsteps.

My mother still tells the story of how, when I was sixteen months old, she was jostled in a crowded department store and momentarily let go of my hand; I seized the opportunity, not to dash away, but to embark upon a brisk but casual stroll around the store. She finally caught up with me—who knows how I got there—at the dry goods counter on another floor. Apparently I responded to the sight of her not with tearful, desperate gratitude, but with something closer to the hail-fellow-well-met greeting Stanley gave Livingstone.

So it's a particular pleasure for me to be Amanda's walking partner. And we *are* partners, in that word's fullest sense. I feel it's a privilege to initiate her into the distinguished order of pedestrians. As far as I'm concerned, a child's self-determination begins when she starts using her legs to make choices, when she literally votes with her feet. Saying, I want to see what this marshy grass feels like under my shoes. Or, I want to stroll over to this dandelion and pull it out of the ground. Or, I want to run over to Daddy and put a hammerlock on his legs.

As a way of describing walking, this might strike you as either cloying or pretentious—or both, maybe. And it is, for adults. But Amanda has never heard the words *cloying* or *pretentious*. However, she intuitively knows the meaning of the word *magical*. And she knows that walking is something magical.

When we're tramping back up the driveway and she points to our house and announces, "Hum! Hum!" sounding for all the world as if she's just spotted port after a month at sea, it's hard for a father not to feel a little enchanted as well.

BURYING MONTY

I'm deeply suspicious of people who form mock-human relationships with their dogs and cats. It is my firm belief that animals were never meant to send or receive birthday cards, wear faux-Burberry raincoats, or be referred to by owners as "my baby." There's something just a shade unsettling about people whose relations with their own species prove so unfulfilling that they come to regard pets as emotional equals.

Having said that, let me admit that our first child was a dog.

Sharon and I were about to be married. One of her longtime friends, Mark, owned a lean and raffish-looking male Akita—a Japanese dog that looks something like a cross between a German shepherd and a husky—who had impregnated a female of the same breed. When Mark asked Sharon what she wanted as a wedding present, she said without hesitation, "One of the puppies." The litter was born about a month following the wedding. About seven weeks after that, Mark brought the runt to our doorstep.

The Saturday Monty entered our lives was one of the most agonizing we had ever endured. Literally. Through some weird newlywed synchronicity, Sharon had undergone root canal work the previous day, less than twenty-four hours after I'd been to an oral surgeon to have an abcessed molar drained. With both of us whirling in a fog composed of equal parts pain, sleep deprivation, and Tylenol with codeine, we were in no shape to greet a puppy. Especially one that was oversized, hyperactive, and displaying a somewhat less than perfect grasp of bladder control.

Even aside from my physical state, I was not entirely enthusiastic about his arrival. Dogs had always been, at best, a matter of indifference to me. And of all the dogs the world offered, the only sort that interested me less than the small, yappy sort was the big, potentially murderous sort—a description very much in line with the Akita reputation.

Sharon counterargued passionately. "Dogs are what you make them," insisted this woman who had never in her life lived with a pet. "Dogs aren't mean unless people turn them mean. If you're loving, they're loving." We newlyweds are known for our willingness to gracefully give in, so that's what I did.

Despite his untamed urinary tract and his predilection for teething on the few pairs of expensive shoes Sharon owned, I fell in love with Monty as quickly as she did—and, of course, being a dog, he returned our sentiments without a second thought. We lavished affection on him, talked to him as if he were a person (though not a very intelligent one), stuffed him with more Snausages than could possibly have been healthy, and delayed the start of discipline until well into his fifth year. We used to joke that he was our test child, the one on whom we could make all our mistakes.

But the truth is, we never had any trouble with him. Perhaps because we couldn't bring ourselves to use physical force as a teaching tool, Monty grew up a committed pacifist, too cheerful and dumb to be a danger to anyone. He must have been a great disappointment to his fellow Akitas.

The three of us developed a repertoire of rituals that wove our lives into a warped approximation of family. It started in the morning, when Monty would curl up in the warm spot left by whoever had gotten out of bed first. (Yes, we should never have allowed it, but we were weak.) On Sundays in pleasant weather, the three of us headed for our neighborhood Irish bar, where in the cheerful little courtyard Sharon and I would nurse Guinnesses while Monty lapped water from a pie tin brought by Marina, his favorite waitress. Each night, he would wait until Sharon and I sat down to our meal before he stuck his nose into his food bowl, which was right beside the table, and began to dispatch the revolting, doughy-smelling beige nuggets he called dinner. Afterward, he and I would walk a route that never varied from night to night. He would even pee on the same lampposts.

We all had each other pegged, as only family does. Sharon and I knew the exact spot he'd be occupying (the kitchen tiles in front of the sink) when we came home from work on a hot afternoon. We also knew we couldn't ever have an animated conversation in bed—an actual argument wasn't necessary—or else Monty would jump up between us and bat his remarkably tiny brown eyes, imploring us to stop.

He, conversely, knew intuitively when our patience with his begging for table scraps was approaching its limit, and when either Sharon or I was in need of a consoling paw on the leg.

Our more or less idyllic threesome continued along for eight years and would doubtless have gone on for at least several more, had Sharon and I not betrayed Monty by conceiving a human child. Even during the early stages of Sharon's pregnancy, he seemed to know that something with ominous consequences for him was happening. I'm not sure what tipped him off—whether he picked up the hormonal changes by sniffing Sharon's skin or whether our treatment of him had changed in some subtle way that he nonetheless detected. But sometimes he would, for no reason, come up to one of us and lick our hand slowly, almost as if he were asking for forgiveness. Then he'd give us a melancholy, questioning look.

As the day of Amanda's birth drew closer, Sharon and I talked to Monty's vet, read magazine articles, picked the brains of other dog owners. We had two goals. One was to make sure that he knew we still loved him, by keeping his life as close as possible to what it had been before the baby. The other was to protect our infant daughter should he decide he didn't like her. It's remarkable, in retrospect, that we didn't see how these two goals canceled each other out.

136

We did everything by the book. When Sharon came home from the hospital after the birth, she entered first, sans Amanda, and gave Monty a big embrace, letting herself be sloshed with his slobber. I tailed Sharon at a moderate distance, tucking our daughter to one side—as if he wouldn't notice, if I were discreet enough, the smuggling of infant contraband into the house. The ruse didn't work. He followed me up into our room and watched me lay her in the bassinet. He then inhaled deeply several times at the foot of her bed. Without any discernible emotion on his face, he left the room.

After Amanda had been around for a few days, Sharon and I tried to initiate, if not a bond, then at least some sort of mutual recognition between the two parties. I'd sit on the floor with the baby on my lap and gently summon Monty over from his traditional spot underneath the coffee table. More often than not, he would glance up at us, then close his eyes again. From time to time, however, he laboriously pulled himself up, trudged over, waved his nose halfheartedly over Amanda's shoulders and face, and then, unmoved, headed off slowly for the kitchen. When she was old enough to have some sense of what was going on around her, she squealed with pleasure at his arrival, lunging for his tail as he sauntered off.

That was about as far as their relationship ever got; Monty's indifference never came close to catching up to Amanda's fascination for him. Still, he didn't show any overt hostility toward her. Sharon and I settled for gratitude over that.

Then, during Amanda's first Christmas Day, Monty did

something he'd never done before. He bit a human being. My mother, who was visiting, dropped a cracker with some guacamole on it near the spot on the floor where he was napping. She stooped down to pick it up. It took half an instant for Monty to growl and strike, leaving a small, deep, jagged puncture wound on her forearm. Hearing the ruckus from the next room, I ran in, saw what had happened, and in a moment of rage and fright started to kick Monty and scream at him—a first for me, too.

Even as I lashed out, I could see a crushed, guilty look in his eyes that made me feel sick inside. Both he and I knew some line had been crossed, some precedent set.

Meanwhile, Sharon and I valiantly attempted to rationalize the incident. It was about food, we told my mother and each other. The food was in his territory. He didn't see my mother often enough to feel comfortable around her. Still, after that day there was a crucial change in our attitude toward Monty. We didn't trust him anymore.

Nonetheless, for months we did a reasonably good job of trying to keep him part of the family. He seemed to realize quite clearly that dire consequences would greet his going after Amanda, so he made avoidance of her his guiding principle. If I walked into the room with her in my arms he'd quietly leave, with only a quick look of reproach to tell me how he felt.

Meanwhile, an unthinkable notion was occurring independently to Sharon and me. Then one night we said it to each other, and the unthinkable became the obvious: He was only a dog.

Pouring our physical and emotional resources into our daughter's wondrous new life, we pretended not to see how unhappy Monty's had become. Part of the bad deal he was getting was a simple matter of logistics; inevitably, the time I spent bouncing around with Amanda on her bedroom floor each morning was subtracted from his walk. But he also caught Sharon and me giving pats and smooches and murmured endearments—things he'd come to expect as his alone—to this interloper. Perhaps worst of all, he must have sensed the tension we felt every time he got close to the baby.

One day in midsummer, the inevitable happened. My sister and her two daughters had come for a visit. The younger of the girls, Allie, was standing in our driveway. Monty suddenly snarled and charged her, teeth bared. Allie hadn't incited him. She wasn't even paying attention to him. He just lost control. Something truly horrible would surely have happened if the leash he was on had been even a foot longer; as it was, his muzzle bruised her upper arm, which was smeared with his saliva.

Allie was merely angry with Monty. The adults, though, were genuinely scared. We knew we'd only just been spared a scene of profound ugliness. We also knew that as long as Monty was around, it was only a matter of time until everyone's luck ended.

Sharon spent a month trying to find a new home for him. We called the ASPCA, the rescue squads it referred her to, the woman who boarded him when we had to go away, anyone we heard of who had a farm. No luck. For a brief time, we considered making him a full-time outdoor dog by installing a run out near the garden, but that seemed like the ultimate exile, even crueler in its way than the alternative that was beginning to seem less and less avoidable: putting him to death.

On a Saturday morning I loaded him into the station wagon and drove to our vet's office. Monty didn't know what was up, I'm sure, but that didn't stop him from issuing his own personal protest; I still smile a little recalling that his final gesture was to whiz on the front wheel of the Miata I parked beside. The receptionist gestured us into a tiny, boxy room with oldish green-and-white linoleum and paneling. It smelled of Pine Sol, mildew, and sick animals. As a place to die, it was one of the more pitiful options. Monty's toenails clicked on the linoleum as he paced—his usual attack of nerves over a routine visit to the vet.

Suddenly, realizing how little he understood, I went from mild queasiness to feeling as if I'd been kicked in the stomach. I wish I could say it felt cathartic to cry, but as I wept I kept thinking: It's all well and good for you to be sobbing like this, but you're still the one who's killing him. The rational voice inside me kept making its point—that there was no other real choice, that Monty would really hurt a child someday and then be put down anyhow. It took all my concentration to keep that voice tuned in.

The weekend vet came in, a soft, pasty-looking guy my age with a neatly barbered jet-black beard. I hated him on sight. However, I couldn't blame him; he was just doing what we'd asked him to do. A nurse strapped a black leather muzzle over Monty's nose and mouth. "I'm sorry," I said to him. "I'm sorry." The vet had me hold Monty's head as he found the vein in the foreleg. This won't be painful, the vet kept saying as he prepared to squeeze the plunger that would release the poison. He said it several more times after he drew the needle out.

He seemed to be right. As I kept holding Monty's head in my arms, stroking his face, what seemed to be happening to his body was not a spasm of agony, but a profound relaxation. His eyes clouded, his breathing grew shallow. He became very heavy. He sighed, and then he was perfectly still.

I was fine—or good enough, anyway—after a few minutes. Spreading out an old, chewed-up blanket that Sharon and I had bought on our honeymoon, I swaddled Monty's body in it, lugged him with some difficulty to the parking lot, and laid him in the rear of the station wagon. It was a peculiarly horrible feeling I had, limp and dissociated at the same time.

Monty and I drove to a willow tree in the field adjacent to our house. There, I dug and dug through the heavy, dun-colored earth, making sure his grave would be deep enough to protect him from predators—he should be spared at least that indignity. It took a very long time before I felt the hole was deep enough. When I was finished, I walked home slowly, washed off the shovel, washed off my shoes, and took a long, hot, soapy shower. Then I dressed in clean clothes, went downstairs, and held my daughter.

For the first week or so I was a dutiful mourner. Sharon couldn't yet face his loss, so I visited Monty's grave alone each night after dinner. However, before long the exercise in penitence started to seem forced and pointless. I stopped going, and I began to wonder: How much had I actually cared about him?

For several months I wrestled with that question, until the October afternoon I was pushing Amanda down the lane behind our house. The air was crisp and vibrant, filled with the smell of apple trees and earth. My daughter was telling herself a rich series of private jokes as the gravel crackled sharply beneath the wheels of her stroller. The fields and the horizon beyond them were etched against the sky with perfect clarity. I thought: Wouldn't it be great to be out on a day like this with Monty?

Almost instantly, as if I'd uttered some magic words, all the tortured logic and emotional anguish of the past year blew away. I saw things in a way that was simple and clear and felt right. I had cared about him, I realized. More than that, I had genuinely loved him. But not as much as any child, not nearly.

He only understood the life we lived before Amanda. It was the only life he was ever capable of understanding. For Sharon and me, on the other hand, little remained from our lives before parenthood. Amanda didn't merely place upon us her immense and justified demands; her presence made us different people, with a different sense of what mattered. She had become, quite simply, our purpose. The way her hands curled over her bottle when she drank, the way she giggled when we played peekaboo from behind the high chair, the way she'd crawl over and pull herself up on my legs, then look up in the expectation of being embraced—those had become the currency of our daily life, not Monty's peculiar and endearing little mannerisms.

Clearly, I now saw, nothing about what had happened was fair to Monty. But it had happened. And I honestly couldn't imagine another, better outcome—at least not one that was even marginally realistic.

From time to time, I still stop by his grave, sit underneath the willow tree, and chat with him for a few minutes. But not about that final year, with its frayed nerves, upheavals, mutual guilt. Instead, he and I reminisce about Marina's charms, and about how good it felt to sit in a bright courtyard on a Sunday afternoon.

THE DAUGHTER TONGUE

You'd never have guessed, from the demure way Amanda entered the world, that today we would be parents to a toddler whose loquacity makes Gracie Allen look like one of those icons from Easter Island. In fact, at the time of delivery the doctor had to give her a pinch to jump-start her crying reflex; up until then, there'd been only a quizzical look and silence.

Today, however, having discovered the power of speech, my daughter rarely comes up for air. And I say that with pride. For her, there is scarcely anything so unremarkable that it deserves to pass without comment—sometimes ten or twenty times consecutively if a parent does not respond immediately. Amanda has turned into the play-by-play announcer for her life, a never-ending game (of what, I'm not quite sure) with a growing roster of players and ever-flashier maneuvers. Personally, I could listen to her for hours. Sometimes I do.

To be honest, it's impossible to pinpoint the moment she uttered her first word, that precise instant when *da-da* and *ma-ma* went from being bewitching nonsense syllables to signifying the two relentlessly doting giants who were always brandishing bottles of formula. I just know that at some point, she made the great leap into language.

I do, however, quite clearly remember her first sentence. It happened one evening as her mother was fixing dinner and Amanda—then fifteen or sixteen months old—was seated on the kitchen floor whirling a piece of string as if it were a miniature lariat. As I stood in the doorway observing her, she suddenly dropped the string, which settled on the floor like a deflated balloon. She put her finger directly in the middle of this droopy configuration and announced, "I see circle."

I was dumbstruck. How did she know what a circle even *was*? (I'm guessing *Sesame Street*.) And how on earth had she made the connection between the flawless circles found in her plastic ring set or her shapes book and the flaccid version she'd created? For the first time in memory, I was amazed by the actual content of something she'd said—not simply by the fact that she'd uttered something intelligible.

Of course, revelatory moments of that sort are commonplace now. It seems anymore that a week can't go by without her figuring out something else she can do with language. She can tell you whether she is hungry, thirsty, happy, or sad—or where it hurts. She can also tell you whether she is playing, jumping, dancing, swimming, hiding, or driving. She knows the names of most of our neighbors, every single child actor on *Barney & Friends,* and a good portion of the animal kingdom. (What gives toddlers this magical recall of animals, anyway? I find it both odd and amazing that an almost-two-year-old who has trouble distinguishing between spinach and cauliflower can immediately spot the difference between a panda bear and a polar bear.)

Now, of course, comes the struggle for understanding, not hers, but ours, as Sharon and I try to take the sense out of our daughter's sometimes less-than-intelligible utterances.

Once Amanda and I were looking at a book when we came to a zoo scene. Amanda was bringing me up to speed on the crucial elements of the tableau—elephants, giraffes, penguins, trees, the balloon vendor—when she said something that I took to be "baby kids." I thought, if she wants to call the children in the picture baby kids, why not? "Yes, baby kids," I said to her.

Instead of being pleased at having been understood, as I would have expected, she continued to repeat the phrase, over and over and over, each time with a sense of mounting frustration. I kept answering back, "Yes, baby kids." Finally she pointed to an infinitesimal object in the lower right-hand corner of the scene. A baby carriage! "Ahh, a baby carriage?" I asked. Amanda was obviously relieved to have penetrated my obtuseness. Still, she said again, "Baby kids," very deliberately, stressing each syllable as if it had just occurred to her that she must make allowances for her father's dull-wittedness.

Interestingly enough, one of the few phrases she hasn't

picked up on—though heaven knows she hears it enough from both her parents—is "I love you." In fact, words that convey affection remain largely absent from her vocabulary, although physical actions that convey affection are lavishly distributed. I used to wonder why Amanda didn't feel obliged to return our verbal assurances of adoration. Now I've come to think she instinctively knows the principle that all great conversationalists live by: Never utter that which is self-evident. Especially when lips and arms can deliver the message far more effectively.

If a child's language is primarily an instrument of pleasure for parents, it can be an instrument of torture, too. The same skill that makes me proud and grateful whenever Amanda says *please* when she wants something and *sankoo* when she gets it also offers occasional glimpses into the unprettier regions of her psyche. I am of course referring here to the two words that chill a parent to the marrow the first time they are heard: "No, mine!"

I won't soon forget the circumstances under which I first heard them. We'd just finished breakfast and I was upstairs brushing my teeth, under Amanda's supervision. I should mention that she has for some time displayed a fascination with dental hygiene that, in an adult, would seem a little kinky; one of the first little tricks she learned after walking was to wobble into the bathroom, yank both Sharon's and my brushes out of the holder, then parade around simultaneously polishing her upper and lower teeth.

She also fetishizes our toothpaste tube, which is why she was attempting to make off with it that morning while I

147

stood by the sink in mid-ablution. I took her hand gently and said, "Please don't take that away, Amanda. The toothpaste has to stay here."

Pulling away from me violently, she snapped, "No, mine! Toopase mine!" She lit out of the bathroom with her booty.

I was determined not to make this a battle of wills. I didn't want to have to pry the goods away from her, so I tried to do a Jimmy Carter. As she sat at the top of the stairs and fiddled with the mouth of the tube, I joined her and tried to negotiate the return of the toothpaste.

I could see right away she was going to be a hard case. Beaming like Dylan Thomas with the first whiskey of the day in front of him, she was engaged in an effort to push her index finger as far as possible into the tube (which luckily wasn't very far). It was a good thing she hadn't yet made the connection between squeezing the tube and getting toothpaste to spurt out. When she retracted her finger, a tiny dab of white dentifrice stuck to its tip—it looked like a miniature Alp. She stuck the finger in her mouth, gasped with delight, and said, "Mmmm! Toopase dishus!" She dipped her finger again, extracting an even smaller amount of toothpaste. Extending the finger to me, she said, with the air of someone handing out free samples of heaven, "Twy it, Daddy."

Tell me *you* wouldn't have folded your cards at this point. But even as I smacked my lips and admired my daughter's skill at preemptive bargaining, that "No, mine!" still rang painfully in my ears. In retrospect, her exercise in self-assertion hasn't proved to be quite the end of innocence I fearfully foresaw at the moment. She was using those words,

I've come to understand, not in order to merely claim a tube of toothpaste, but to claim her share of the world.

It's no accident that she uses "No, mine!" only to protect the really cherished objects in her life—her stuffed dog, her coloring books—or to appropriate those things that her parents find a little too interesting, like the laptop computer on which Daddy is writing his book. In other words, things that define her, either by surrounding or by excluding her. It's the same impulse that makes her say, "No, no!" when she sees Sharon and me hugging in the kitchen; all she sees is that she's not being hugged, too.

In truth, so far she says "No, mine!" far less often than I was convinced she would. Granted, hearing it always touches an exposed nerve. But over time I've come to see her use of the possessional imperative in the same manner that I see every other aspect of my daughter's ever-deepening talent for putting her life into words. It's just one more way she lets us know, every single day, that she is growing into the world.

THE BOY NEXT DOOR

Had you asked me, in the days immediately following Amanda's birth, what my probable attitude toward her future beaus would be, you'd have received an instant, clear-cut response: barely disguised suspicion bordering on surliness. As patently unreasonable as it was, I couldn't help but feel my daughter offered potential suitors infinitely more than they could ever offer in return.

And, after all, having been a teenage boy in extremis at one point in my life, I knew exactly what teenage boys were up to. A phrase containing the words *no* and *good* suggested itself.

However, now, roughly a year and a half into Amanda's life, my resolve to protect my little girl against my fellow cavemen has already weakened. In other words, she has a boyfriend. And I find myself sort of hoping their relationship stays as it is for the next, say, twenty years. Of course, it's axiomatic that these early love affairs meet their doom in fairly short order. But one can always hope that this time, things will be different.

Max is, literally, the boy next door. At this age they often are, I understand. When she sees him from afar, she gets this look of expectancy in her eyes and calls, "Masss, Masss" (her *x* needs a little polish) and dashes off toward him, looking like one of those Navy wives on the World War II newsreels sprinting to their uniformed husbands as the boat debarks. Amanda is, of course, too young to play it cool. (As a writer I know once observed, one of the great things about toddlers is that they are sometimes hot and sometimes cold, but *never* cool.)

Max is seven weeks older than she is, a brooding, chunky, square-shouldered blond with deep-set eyes of a pale blue that can, in certain lights, appear lavender. Not that you should think for a moment that Amanda's attraction to him is merely physical. She may barely be able to string a three-word sentence together, but she's not shallow. I know exactly what she sees in him. Though he has not yet reached his second birthday, you can look into those eyes and tell exactly what kind of person he'll grow up to be: decent, methodical, patient, tolerant, affectionate. All in all, not bad material for a life partner.

If she's attracted to him, he's crazy about her. If his adoring gaze and his habit of picking dandelions for her (he has no doubt seen his father give his mother flowers) aren't enough of a tip-off, his clumsy and frequent attempts to en-wrap my daughter in his manly arms pretty much clinch the deal.

You couldn't exactly call Max and Amanda soulmates, but they do complement each other as well as many adult couples I know. Theirs is a friendship uncontaminated by ulterior motives, ambition, a sense of appropriate boy or girl behavior, or indeed by any expectations whatsoever. When they're together, Max and Amanda take their cues from nothing except each other.

I challenge any adult to spend fifteen minutes in the same room with them and emerge from the experience still claiming that kids this age are too young to care about their peers. Sure, they're both subject to the toddler's basic self-absorption, but that's something they accept in each other. If Max doesn't want Amanda putting a stuffed bear on his bicycle, he grunts disapprovingly and she backs off without a fuss. If she's not of a mind to smooch with him, she gives him one of those I-need-oxygen squeals. (Just like she does with me, in fact.) He takes the hint.

If you accept the term "sharing" in a loose sense, they share. For toddlers, what this means is that each doesn't automatically want what the other has. Even their juice cup is communal, and they defy any adult's efforts to have it otherwise. And in fact their sharing goes beyond the physical; sometimes they seem tapped into some preverbal form of communication—which it would have to be, as Max is not yet talking much. I have seen them, while pursuing separate recreations on the patio, look up at each other at the same moment, exchange a glance, and suddenly tear off simultaneously in the same direction, as if some supersonic starting gun audible only to toddlers had just been fired.

Sharon thinks Amanda bosses Max around. I think she looks out for him. Take the time that she kept saying, "No, Masss," as he tried to pull the lining out of his older brother's bicycle helmet. She wasn't, it seemed to me, attempting to run Max's life, but trying to keep a buddy from the consequences of a rash act. (She might also have been protecting the property of the older brother, Douglas, whom she idolizes but seems to view as a figure slightly out of reach, like some kind of movie star. He is, after all, seven.)

"Max and Amanda," Sharon once mused. "Sounds like somebody's grandparents." And so it does. And in fact they sometimes do seem like an old married couple, especially when they're puttering around together inside the playhouse on Max's patio. He contemplatively bangs a plastic hammer against the wall. She examines a stray Dr. Seuss book. They are essentially independent, yet easy in each other's company.

I realized how much they meant to each other this past Fourth of July, when we had a cookout with Max's family. At one point, he and I were playing with his miniature but very powerful battery-operated mag-wheeled monster truck. I thought it might be interesting to divert the truck's path so that it rumbled over his legs, up his torso, and across his chest. Max naturally found this immensely amusing, more so even than crashing the vehicle into the nearest wall; he expressed his pleasure with the low-pitched, strangled laugh that is his signature. Amanda immediately heard it and came running over. Suddenly, as far as both of them were concerned, having a monster truck drive all over you was just the thing.

Nothing unusual there in terms of toddler behavior. What made the incident remarkable to me was seeing their mutual willingness to take turns—a social nicety that usually eludes Amanda when she's playing with other toddlers. For her to relish this moment, it wasn't necessary for the tire tracks to be on her knees. Max's pleasure triggered hers.

Just this morning, she arose a little before six-thirty and called from her bedroom to ours, "Wake up, Daddy." I retrieved her and brought her downstairs en route to the kitchen. I was envisioning our morning in terms of a nice cup of milk, then perhaps a retreat to the living room to rummage through the toy basket (and maybe for Daddy to nap on the couch for a few minutes). But Amanda had other ideas. "Down," she informed me as we passed the front door. "Walk."

"Walk?" I asked. "You couldn't want to go for a walk *now*. It's too early."

"Masss," she said, and reached for the doorknob.

"No, sweetie. Max is asleep," I said. "You can see Max later."

In the space of several seconds, she went through a repertoire of anguish that Joan Crawford would have been hard pressed to equal. First came astonishment, then despair, then rage. She went crimson and wailed raw-throatedly, desperately. Tears spurted from her eyes as if they were lined up waiting to get out. I don't think her display of emotion was simple willfulness, or manipulation, or a preview of The Terrible Twos. I just think she wanted to be with her boyfriend, even if it was six-thirty in the morning.

I also think this thing with boys is going to get very tricky when she's about ten years older.

THE TELLTALE HEART

I felt a virus coming on and I left work early. So it was strictly by chance that I was at home, sprawled on the couch, when Sharon brought Amanda back from her one-year checkup. Listening to the story behind my unexpected presence, my wife expressed the requisite surprise and sympathy, but her manner seemed perfunctory. I found this a bit off-putting, to be honest. When your spouse touches your forehead with her fingertips and says, "Poor baby," you don't want her to sound as if she's phoning it in. You want her to give it some emotion. I mean, being a sick patriarch ought to count for something.

She slipped Amanda's jacket off, cradled her as she knocked back a bottle of apple juice, then carried our daughter upstairs to her afternoon nap, all with that patented, offhand air of motherly competence. When she came back downstairs, she put her arms around me and started to shudder. She inhaled sharply and was quite clearly fighting back tears.

This wasn't precisely what I expected.

"What's wrong?" I said softly, then a couple of times more insistently. She held me fiercely. It took her a minute or so to catch her breath.

When she did she said, "It's her heart."

A vague feeling of nausea that had nothing to do with the virus welled up in my stomach. "What about her heart?"

"Dr. Murray heard something funny when he listened to it. He said it sounded like a squeak." She shuddered again.

"What did he say about this squeak?" I said. I was trying to keep my tone of voice level. I sensed that my assigned part in all this was to act the clear-eyed, problem-solving, tell-me-exactly-what-happened partner. For this I was grateful, because having to practice emotional restraint was pretty much the only thing keeping me from dissolving into panic. "Did he think it might be a heart murmur?" I asked the question because I knew Sharon had a mild one, and also because it was probably the least horrifying of the available alternatives.

Putting a specific, concrete question to Sharon seemed to compose her. "He said maybe. He isn't sure. He said it didn't sound quite like any murmur he'd ever heard. But still . . . there's a good chance that's what it is."

"What is he going to do about it?"

"He wants us to set up a chest X-ray and an EKG as soon

as possible." A small, mordant smile appeared at the corners of her mouth. "He told us not to worry until he sees the results. That should be easy, right?" She held me again, and then her tears began in earnest.

"It's okay," I said gently. "She's going to be okay." Originality in a crisis isn't exactly my strong suit. Luckily, at that moment, no talent mattered less.

When her crying stopped after a minute or so, Sharon said, more to herself than to me, "I just wanted her to be perfect."

"She is," I whispered.

I told Sharon to grab a little nap. Not long after she lay down, I slipped into Amanda's bedroom. Just at that moment, I needed to look at my daughter's sleeping profile and to meditate. As always, the outlines of her round, infinitely peaceful face held everything that mattered to me. Serene, rhythmically inhaling small lungfuls of life, she was flawless and complete and ravishing. In a word, perfect. Or so I would have thought a half hour before.

In the morbid way of someone who has always been suspicious of good luck—and what luckier thing had ever happened than Amanda?—this day was one I'd been half expecting for all of her short life. The Moment of Payback, the Big Oh-by-the-Way. Few parents we knew had been spared it. Not the Lamaze-mates whose year-old daughter spent New Year's Day in a Puerto Rican hospital with a fever that put her near death and a team of doctors who couldn't figure out what her symptoms meant. Not the friends whose gorgeous, thoughtful six-year-old son had been diagnosed with juvenile diabetes the previous summer.

And especially not Spencer's parents. Perpetually amused, fearless, one of my favorite children, Spencer had died at the age of eight months as the result of a congenital heart problem. At his viewing, I couldn't decide which was more painful, seeing him in an open coffin (the family was devoutly Catholic) or having his parents come up to the mourners and chipperly ask how work was going while pretending they hadn't been torn to bits by the loss of their son.

Certainly it's more than a little narcissistic to view your child's illness as your own misfortune. Still, in every case of this kind that I know, the child has been amply endowed with whatever emotional resources were needed to deal with his or her medical realities. It's the parents who fall apart. And now it was our turn—perhaps—to take a spin in the tragedy machine. I was even more poorly prepared than I would have figured on being.

It's a silly male thing, I know, but from the instant Amanda was born I'd felt in my heart that I was somehow her protector. In those first days I found myself on several occasions gazing upon her and muttering under my breath, "If anyone ever tried to hurt you. . . ." (Not that anyone had expressed the remotest interest in such a thing.) It was as if the mere sight of her entering the world had activated some strange gland and a hormone had been released, making me acutely sensitive to the potential presence of predators and other forms of mortal danger. Very handy if you live in the Pleistocene Era or the East Village, but not ultimately all that practical in suburbia.

In those early days, I had recurring—and embarrassingly trite—fantasies about saving Amanda's life. The situations were straight out of standard melodrama; I'd be escaping a burning building with her in my arms, or catching her just before she fell from a clifftop. I chalked these daydreams up to the low-level postpartum weirdness that new fathers, in their own particular way, seem to go through. In time the fantasies waned, though the feeling that set them off never completely disappeared.

Ironically, now that danger really *had* arrived, the first truth to sink in was how little I could actually do. As I watched Amanda snooze away in oblivious bliss, the alternatives presently before Sharon and me seemed bleakly obvious. The three of us could hang together as we ran the gauntlet of doctors and technicians and cold tiled rooms. And I could pray like mad. That pretty much summed up the options.

Amanda's chest X-ray was quickly taken care of—I came home from work one evening the following week and Sharon told me she'd had it done that afternoon. But the EKG proved a problem. The local clinics, we quickly discovered, were booking a minimum of three weeks in advance. Dr. Murray was leaving for a month's vacation in a week and a half. It went without saying we wouldn't wait six weeks to find out the condition of our daughter's heart. Finally, by imposing on the husband of a friend who worked there, Sharon managed to get a Saturday-morning appointment at a hospital an hour away, in a bleak, burnt-out industrial city I hadn't been forced to see in years.

As if to underscore how little control we had over anything in our lives, when we arrived in the city we found that our friend's directions to the hospital were useless. We spent at least twenty minutes circling the largely boarded-up business district and were about to be late when, quite by accident, I happened to spot the hospital's sign, down the street from an intersection we'd just driven through.

I know that in the cosmic scheme of things, thousands of things more fairly deserve the label of tragedy than a child being wheeled by a parent down the drab gray-and-white linoleum corridors of a hospital on her way to a simple medical test. I told myself there was every reason to believe things would turn out fine. My child wasn't one of the millions of children on this earth who have been drained of hope by war or famine or abuse or poverty. She simply had a funny heartbeat that was, in all likelihood, meaningless. However, knowing this didn't make me any less frightened when the jovially detached nurse-technician stuck Amanda's tiny naked chest with adhesive-backed metal coins trailing multicolored wires, which she plugged into a forbidding, six-foot-tall, steel-gray piece of technology that looked as if it required a pilot's license to operate.

Perhaps predictably, Amanda was barely ruffled by the strange room, the strange woman, the strange machinery. The novelty of the hospital, the nurse's professionally dispensed baby talk, the fluorescent screens and colored lights (so reminiscent of Daddy's stereo), all came in for her intense scrutiny. It was almost a relief when, toward the end of the procedure, impatient at having to stay still so long, Amanda started to fuss. Sharon and I practically fought for the right to comfort her.

Upon escaping the hospital, we had an odd urge to linger in this horrible city; my suspicion is that we both realized that as soon as we reached home, The Wait would officially begin. Stalling, we circled the downtown until we saw a storefront Caribbean restaurant called the Sunny Day. Both our antennae went up. It looked tatty but cheerful. With any luck, it would live up both to its name and to its aura.

And it did. Amanda delightedly stuffed shreds of dense West Indian–style bread in her mouth while her mother and I tucked into a pepper pot soup that took us back to the time we spent in Jamaica not long after we were married. The waitress swore our little girl was the prettiest thing she'd seen in months. From a tape player in the kitchen, Toots and the Maytals were singing that goofy reggae version of "Louie Louie." As the soup made a hollow of warmth in my stomach, I was struck by a thought that hadn't even occurred to me in the weeks since we first heard about Amanda's heart: maybe things would be okay. I even said this, out loud, to Sharon as we were driving home. She looked at me and gave me a half nod, smiling tentatively.

I mention this lunch mostly because it's indicative of what the two of us put ourselves through emotionally over the next six days, while we waited for the test results. In the absence of any concrete knowledge, we relied on omens. A good bowl of pepper pot soup or an easy morning commute meant a favorable outcome on Amanda's tests. A stain on a tie or a window cracked by a tree branch during a storm portended a larger blow to come.

Sharon and I went to sleep every evening talking sensibly, hopefully; in the morning we would wake up in knots, for no reason other than that during the night we'd both had a chance to dream our fears. We kept repeating to each other—as if the words alone would cast the proper spell—that neither of the technicians had seen anything to arouse their suspicions. Then I silently reminded myself that neither of these technicians was, in point of fact, qualified to interpret anything she'd seen.

Meanwhile, there was nothing Amanda's self-appointed protector could do about anything. Looking at her, normally the easiest thing in the world for me to do, had suddenly sprouted complications. Understanding that we might lose her—almost certainly wouldn't, I kept saying, but *might*—gave her a dimension, a gravity I hadn't seen before. If I'd ever been unclear about how ardently, how deeply I loved my daughter, I was unclear no longer. Yet, at the same time, the sight of her kept reminding me just how little control I had over her, or anything.

Needless to say, I wasn't much of a playmate for the near week that we waited. When your father's job is to roll the ball across the carpet and squeal along with you, you don't want him drinking you in with a look of foreboding instead.

One night I found myself praying and promising God I would do anything at all in exchange for my daughter's health. The only thing that mattered was that she be allowed to live. But then I remembered the liberatingly generous, yet implacable truth: God doesn't do deals. God gives. And He chooses what it is He gives—just as He chose to give us our daughter in the first place. This realization didn't help as much as it should have.

I wish I could remember more about the period of waiting. One of the few things I do recall is getting more deeply immersed than usual in my job. This was, I am fully aware, a coward's response. But when you're feeling your helplessness all too keenly, one way of coping is to fall back on what you know you do well. For men, all too often, what we do well is our daily work. It's finally a pretty dumb way of dealing with heartache, though far from the dumbest.

I also remember that I didn't say a whole lot about Amanda's condition to anyone. If it came up at all, it was in passing—as something I felt Sharon might be a little too worried about. I, of course, knew everything would be fine, though it would obviously be good to get the results back just so my wife's mind would be at ease. More spinelessness? Of course.

Late Friday morning the telephone rang at my desk. When I picked it up, Sharon said, "Hi, darling. She's okay."

Part of me wanted to shout with happiness, but another part felt a little reluctant to dismiss my carefully nursed anxiety quite so quickly. "What does *okay* mean, exactly?" I asked.

"Dr. Murray says that what she's got is called an innocent murmur."

Innocent murmur. The phrase had a certain poetry. Still, not quite ready to believe at that moment that all our fears had been instantly swept aside, I spent another couple of minutes asking Sharon all the implications of an innocent murmur—would it affect Amanda's activities in any way, could it become a problem later on, was there anything we should be looking for, was Dr. Murray going to keep tabs on it? Sharon assured me that although he would of course maintain a close watch, Dr. Murray's answers indicated that our daughter was the absolute picture of health.

"I knew it all along," I said lightly.

"Sure," Sharon said. "Just like I did."

For lunch, I went to the Irish bar across the street and ordered a hamburger and a pint of Guinness. It's something of a superstition of mine that when good fortune makes its presence known in a blindingly obvious way, it's a good idea to offer up a private toast to God. The beer arrived, and I tipped the glass discreetly toward the heavens and thanked Him for keeping my child safe from harm. And also for at least considering her protector's prayers, while also putting her protector gently in his place.

At her eighteen-month checkup, Dr. Murray put his stethoscope to Amanda's chest again. He heard nothing but the sturdy thump of a heart that functioned perfectly.

REENTER AMANDA

On Saturday I wake to the muted patter of a light drizzle on the maple tree outside our bedroom window. As my senses gradually come to their senses, there's more: the smell of the lawn cut yesterday; the aftershave-blue readout of the clock radio (6:52) against the half-gray backdrop of morning light; Sharon's shallow breathing and reassuring aroma, a little like a loaf of bread that's just come out of the oven, but much sexier. However, most of all there is the music of Amanda, who is twittering to herself in the next room.

Not prepared to stir just yet, I half focus on my daughter's distant soliloquy. It's mostly gibberish, practice for real conversation. It sounds like a cross between Swedish and scat singing. As it rises and falls in volume, from time to time I'll catch a stray phrase: ". . . da mommies, da daddies, da mom-

mies, da daddies . . ." or *"Yesssss!* Da bafroom!" Or there will
be a half minute of silence, broken by a squealed "Yikes!"
and a collusive giggle. As I listen, I contemplate the restora-
tive possibilities of remaining suspended in this moment for,
oh, a couple of months.

Actually, the moment lasts longer than I would have dared
hope—almost twenty minutes according to the clock radio,
though in this dreamy state it feels closer to an hour. Then,
after one of her extended silences, the words I've been expecting waft gently, sweetly from bedroom to bedroom:
"Daddy, where *aahhhh* you? Oh, Daddy . . ."

This day, I already have a feeling, is going to be one of
the delicious ones.

I slip on a T-shirt and gym shorts and make my entrance.
Amanda is upright, clutching the railing. She's expecting me.
Her chestnut curls career from her head like sofa springs
gone mad, her eyes glitter in the half-light. One hand has
been swallowed by the sleeve of her yellow pajamas. She
squeezes her greeting into a single breathless word, "Hidaddy, hidaddy." Then a little jump, and the arms held out
theatrically. "Up, please?" She has only recently added the *l*
to this last word, and she shows off her new linguistic ex-
pertise by giving the sound extra stress.

Lifting her out of the crib, I press my child's twenty-two-
month-old body to my chest. She is so soft, so substantial, so
at ease in my embrace. She clamps onto me like I'm a mag-
net, wrapping her legs around my sides. Could there be any
doubt that this is the real thing, Plato's "grave mental dis-
ease"—in other words, capital-L Love? I bury my nose in her

167

hair, which is still fluffy and fresh-smelling from last night's shampoo, and murmur, "Can Daddy have a kiss?"

"No," she says decisively, though not unkindly. It's simply that there's too much else that requires her immediate attention. "Down, please," she says, wriggling for emphasis. I place her on the floor and she tears off for our room.

"Amanda, wait," I half whisper, half call. "Mommy's sleeping."

"Mommy seeping," she repeats as she barrels through the doorway. (The *l* hasn't made it into all her words.) "Wake *up*, Mommy. Wake *up*." Amanda fetches up right beside the expanse of mattress I have recently vacated and spreads her arms across the bed, pushing off her tiptoes and trying to get some leverage by corkscrewing her rear end upward. "Up on da bed," she calls to me, using the flat, no-nonsense tone of a woman who expects service. "Up on da bed, *please*." There's no disobeying *that* voice.

Sharon has somehow, luckily for her, managed to wake up before the assault begins. I slip into bed alongside the rest of my family. Amanda's under the comforter, kicking her legs like a fledgling karate master and cackling. After roughly a half minute of truly inspirational snuggling, my daughter turns to me. "Juice, please?" she says.

"How about some milk?" I ask her.

"Okay," she quickly replies.

"I'll get you some milk, then," I say. But I am not in much of a hurry to leave; nuzzling the back of my daughter's neck is a much more interesting idea. Not to her, though. "No, Daddy," she says brusquely. "Go 'way."

"Yeah, Daddy," Sharon says mock indignantly. "Can't you see you're bothering us? Go get the milk."

So I do. "Sankoo, Daddy," Amanda says briskly when I return and hand her the lidded cup. I've also fetched coffee and the morning newspaper from the driveway—have you noticed what a useful guy I am?—and so the three of us burrow in. Or two of us do, at any rate. It doesn't take Amanda long to become impatient with her parents' shortsighted desire to bury their noses in newsprint. She hits on an ingenious way to recapture our attention. She grabs the sports section and announces, "I reading."

"Yes, I can see that," I say, grateful for an opportunity not to learn exactly how the Orioles lost again. "You're reading the paper."

"I reading da paper."

"Indeed you are."

A pause. "Mommy's paper. Daddy's paper."

"That's right. And Amanda's paper, too."

This draws a chortle. " 'Manna's paper. 'Manna read da paper," she exclaims as if her talents were a never-ending source of surprise and delight even to herself. Turning her attention back to the boxscores, she mimes literacy for a half minute, then decides she is better suited to a life of action.

Before very long the news of the day can no longer compete with my daughter's exhibition of squirming, diving, and pouncing, which appears to be composed of equal parts modern dance and Thai boxing. There is also, around this time, a suspicious odor coming from her pajama bottoms. Sharon says, "You take care of your friend's diaper and I'll get breakfast going." This strikes me as a very sound deal—for Sharon, too, because I am acknowledged house-wide as a master diaper changer. Only I know the secret of keeping Amanda from shimmying down off the day bed and turning each change into an episode of *The Fugitive*.

The secret? You've got to know the enemy's weakness. Amanda's is Baby Magic lotion. Don't ask me what she sees in it—possibly the violently pink color, or that peculiar odor that reminds me for some reason of raisins. All I know is that she's nutty for the stuff. Even as I'm starting to pull the old diaper off, I wave the plastic bottle before her eyes. She reaches for it. "Losun, please," she begs.

"You'll have to wait," I say. "Just for a moment." But I'm no tease. Between each segment of the change—after the wipe, after the balm, after the new diaper—I squirt a Rice Krispie–size dab of lotion into her palm. She eyes it for a moment, sniffs it to make sure it's genuine, then rubs it vigorously onto her stomach.

Until breakfast is ready, Amanda and I color. Actually, it started with trying to convince her that my filling in the crossword puzzle was a form of parallel-play coloring. This selling job proved too successful; she is now happily defacing the funny pages with an orange crayon while I try to feign interest in a coloring book inhabited by generic-looking cartoon forest creatures. (Though, in truth, this owl does look kind of cool in bright red. . . .)

When the chow arrives, Amanda's captivated by our pancakes, unmoved by her own. I think it has a lot to do with Mommy and Daddy being kitted out with forks and knives while she has been served a bowl of precut squares slightly bigger than postage stamps. "Daddy pancake," she demands, grabbing for it. The gloves are off now. No *please.*

"Daddy's eating his pancake. You eat your pancake," I tell her calmly but in no uncertain terms, knowing full well that the first tears of the morning are about to be shed. The storm is brief but intense; Sharon limits the damage by taking one of the pancake squares, dipping it into the dregs of the maple syrup on her own plate, and placing it into Amanda's mouth. Suddenly, our daughter realizes, her breakfast has acquired a purpose. She hands the squares, one by one, to her mother for the ceremonial dipping into the leftover syrup.

Sated, she gears up for our customary Saturday-morning post-breakfast walk. As I transfer her from high chair to floor, she says, "Come on, Daddy," and starts for the front door.

"Not today, sweetie," I say. "It's raining outside." I take her to the door to show her.

"Da waining?" she asks disconsolately.

"Yes, sweetie, I'm sorry." She takes my hand and moves it toward the doorknob anyway. Certainly a *macher* like her dad can have a few rainclouds gotten out of the way.

"No, Amanda," I try to explain. "I know you want to take a walk, but we can't go right now. It's raining."

Suddenly the rain outside seems like nothing—in our foyer, a Force 5 gale has been unleashed. Amanda goes crimson, her face twists into a Kabuki-like mask of fury, the air is rent by her agonized screeches. Worse yet, in the process of stamping her feet she loses her balance and plops ignominiously on her bum, so that humiliation is added to rage.

I kneel and offer her my arms. She comes to me and holds on tight, nestling her head on my shoulder and patting my back, as if I am the one in need of solace. From the beginning to the end of this scene, perhaps forty-five seconds have elapsed.

"We'll take a walk later, after the rain," I tell her consolingly. "Right now, I think *Sesame Street* is on." Okay, television is a lazy parent's recourse. Nonetheless, the way we spectate together—I bounce her on my knee to a country-and-western song about recycling or something, we run through the alphabet, very approximately, with Elmo—feels more like play than paralysis. She settles in my arms and glances over her shoulder, fixing me with a conspiratorial look that says, "That little show I put on a couple of minutes ago? We both know I didn't mean it, right? I've been under some stress lately, and. . . ." Well, what are fathers for, if not to be on the receiving end of a little hissy fit now and again?

After the show's over, we play with some contraption that resembles a one-armed bandit except that every time you pull the lever a scratchy voice says something about colors. It's not exactly Graham Greene or *The Red and the Black;* still, she's fixated by it, so I'm willing to play along. When the novelty of this gizmo wears off, we look through her *Life-size Book of Animals* together. But before long I notice that she's starting to get the faraway look and heavy, clumsy movements of a child for whom nap time is within collapsing distance. Sure enough, she breaks off from an authoritative discourse on which baby animals belong to which mommies, leaning her head on my thigh. "Is it nap time?" I ask.

"No," she says. Then, with a sigh that is part resignation, part gratitude, "Okay."

Remarkably, she goes down for the count almost instantly, but not before insisting that I hug her through the slats of the crib. "Bye, Daddy. See you soon," she sighs, and she's out. As I stand above her crib I recall, for the second or third time this week, the day we lowered her into it for the first time. Her throw-pillow-sized body curled into a corner of the linens and was almost swallowed up; we wondered how she would ever grow into her bedding. Now, stretched to her full length, she reaches more than halfway from one end of the mattress to the other. She looks like a giantess.

Back downstairs, in the ensuing calm, I get to devour the newspaper for real and even have the opportunity to share an actual cup of hot coffee with Sharon. But I keep seeing that long, lean form floating off to sleep.

"How could two years scoot by so quickly?" I ask Sharon.

"Time flies when you're shell-shocked," she says wryly.

Not long afterward, Sharon heads upstairs to grab a few minutes' more sleep, and I have the house to myself. By now the rain is falling steadily outside, drumming on the gutters, spattering against the gravel. Sprawled on the couch, I try to finish the crossword puzzle, but the orange crayon marks have rendered that idea a non-starter. No matter. I sit back and stretch, and as I do I feel the ghost on my chest of where I held Amanda just a few minutes before.

She's almost two. It's almost inconceivable, and yet there you are. Twenty-two months ago you were nestling a motionless infant under your armpit. Now you are watching her take the three steps down from your front porch—and doing

173

it solo. You're holding out a hand so that when she polishes off her plum, she can nonchalantly hand you the pit. You're reading her not just any book, but the one she asks for by name.

And, most remarkably, the two of you are starting to have real conversations. These are not always pleasant—Amanda is not one to take a parent's disobedience lightly—but they're vastly more fulfilling than baby talk. When you discover that it's actually possible to communicate with your child, to get across your ideas and desires and impressions of the world, the relationship shifts into a higher gear. And if all this astounds you, imagine how it must seem to her.

I'd never been a guy who thought much about the future before becoming a father. (My bank book bears eloquent testimony to this fact.) Now it's something I think about a lot, usually with a feeling that's not so much fear as . . . suspense, I suppose. This is no doubt why I've been talking lately to a few guys I know whose kids are a little older than Amanda. The exercise has proved helpful—not just for the advice, but for the reassuring news that my friends' appetite for fatherhood remains as lusty as it was back in its own infancy.

Robert, whose daughter just turned six, said not long ago, "Rosie really has her own life now. That must sound like we're not as close as we were back when she was a toddler. In fact, I feel like we're closer. She really tells us what she feels and thinks now, and she asks really wonderful questions. To be honest about it, just about any guy could have changed her diaper and she probably wouldn't have known the difference. But now I feel like I'm the only guy who could *really* be her father."

My friend David, whose son is now eight, told me, "I enjoy Riley more than I ever have, because I feel I'm getting to know him just as he's getting to know himself. And the older he gets, the more there is to his life. When he was a baby, I couldn't imagine anything better. When he was a toddler, I said to Sally, 'Two is definitely the best age.' But I ended up saying the same thing when he was three and four and so on. I still feel that way. It just gets better."

Right this minute, as I laze on the couch, listening distractedly to the rain and suddenly realizing that wherever I look in our living room, there's a toy chest or a Barney book or a small stray sock, I feel very strongly that almost two is definitely the best age. So far, anyway.

Maybe, it occurs to me, David's optimism is the ultimate realism as well. Is it honestly possible that as time goes on, the pleasure I take in fatherhood will grow even richer? That a man could enjoy his children even more as they grow up? After a morning like this, it doesn't seem possible that things could get any better, and yet . . .

"Mommeee, Daddeee . . ." Though faint, Amanda's voice pulls me back to earth. I'm being cued.

"Daddy will be upstairs in just a minute," I call, taking the steps two at a time.

ABOUT THE AUTHOR

BILL MCCOY is a senior editor at *Parents* magazine. A native of Pennsylvania, he is a graduate of Pennsylvania State University and the University of Iowa. He lives with his wife and daughter outside Princeton, New Jersey.